I0146555

Index to

Rutherford County, Tennessee,

Wills and Administrations

1804—1861

Byron Sistler and Barbara Sistler

JANAWAY PUBLISHING, INC.
Santa Maria, California

Copyright © 1990 by Byron Sistler and Associates, Inc.

ALL RIGHTS RESERVED. Written permission must be secured from the
author or the publisher to use or reproduce any part of this book,
in any form or by any means, including electronic reproduction,
except for brief quotations in critical reviews or articles.

Originally Published:
Nashville, Tennessee
1990

Reprinted by

Janaway Publishing, Inc.
732 Kelsey Ct.
Santa Maria, California 93454
(805) 925-1038
www.JanawayGenealogy.com

2006, 2013

ISBN: 978-1-59641-037-4

Made in the United States of America

INDEX TO
RUTHERFORD COUNTY, TENNESSEE
WILLS & ADMINISTRATIONS 1804 TO 1861

This index covers all record books (will books) from 1804 through 1861. The entries were taken directly from microfilm of the original books. They are relatively self-explanatory, but a few observations are in order:

> The year shown is, where possible, year of the probate. Otherwise year of the will, or first year mention is found of the estate.

> At the end of each entry is identification where the instrument can be found--rb (Record Book) followed by book # and page number. For example, rb-17-360 means Record Book 17 page 360.

> In general we attempted to insert notation regarding an estate only once, when it first appeared in the records. Exceptions were (1) if there was an actual will, the page number was shown even if there was a previous entry for that estate; (2) if a later insertion had been found with a more complete name--name instead of initials, etc.--or a substantially different spelling of what seemed to be the same name; (3) if ten years or more had passed since last entry for that name.

Guardian proceedings and settlements are to be found sprinkled throughout the books. While these contain much data of genealogical value, we omitted these references as not within the scope of this particular work.

Where a book had two series of pagination--starting over with page 1 somewhere in the middle, for example--we have marked the second set of page numbers with an asterisk.

Byron Sistler
Barbara Sistler

Nashville, TN
August 1990

Abernathy, Mary 1855 rb-17-360

Adam, William 1832 rb-8-470

Adcock, John 1822 rb-5-237

Adkerson, A. G. 1856 rb-18-131

Adkerson, James 1854 rb-16-706

Adkerson, James E. 1854 rb-17-191

Adkinson, A. G. 1858 rb-19-464

Adkinson, Eliza 1857 rb-18-557

Adkinson, William 1855 rb-17-548

Ailor, George 1848 rb-14-217

Ailor, Jourden 1848 rb-14-465

Alexander, Daniel 1857 rb-19-79

Alexander, Elexis 1816 rb-3-189

Alexander, John 1829 rb-8-10

Alexander, Levi 1831 rb-8-235

Alexander, Pritchett 1860 rb-20-466

Alexander, William 1818 rb-4-187

Alexander, William R. 1849 rb-15-187

Allen, Eli 1860 rb-20-686

Allison, James 1849 rb-15-9

Allison, Nancy 1849 rb-15-1

Alor, George 1848 rb-14-336

Alor, Jordan 1848 rb-14-423

Alor, Joseph 1848 rb-14-423

Anderson, Geo. W. jr. 1851 rb-15-587

Anderson, George 1853 rb-16-538

Anderson, Henry C. 1852 rb-16-241

Anderson, Jackson 1837 rb-9-458

Anderson, Mansfield 1858 rb-19-156

Anderson, Mansfield G. 1860 rb-20-389

Anderson, Mansfield Y. 1859 rb-20-106

Anderson, Samuel 1860 rb-20-476

Anderson, George W. 1848 rb-14-390

Anderson, Samuel 1859 rb-20-184

Anderson, William 1840 rb-10-622

Andrews, James 1814 rb-2-304

Andrews, John (esq.) 1808 rb-2-40

Andrews, John 1812 rb-2-188

Andrews, John 1813 rb-2-271

Anthony, John 1836 rb-9-374

Anthony, Zephenia H. B. 1846 rb-13-690

Anthony, Frances 1836 rb-9-363

Anthony, John 1825 rb-6-122

Arbuckle, Joseph 1821 rb-5-135

Arbuckle, Joseph 1832 rb-8-463

Armstrong, Samuel 1832 rb-8-468

Arnold, Asa 1836 rb-9-373

Arnold, Elenor 1860 rb-20-422

Arnold, James 1808 rb-2-58

Arnold, John 1824 rb-6-6

Arnold, John 1837 rb-10-58

Arnold, John W. 1839 rb-10-540

Arnold, William (Capt) 1857 rb-19-180

Arnold, William 1814 rb-2-291

Arnold, William 1857 rb-19-43

Arnold, John W. 1840 rb-10-481

Ashman, Lewis 1821 rb-5-157

Atkinson, Edward 1856 rb-18-187

Atkinson, Sarah 1858 rb-19-427

Atkinson, Wm. 1853 rb-16-711

Atkinson, James 1854 rb-16-704

Atwood, Elender 1826 rb-6-225

Audres, John 1820 rb-5-31

Backary, Elizabeth 1840 rb-10-509

Baird, Adam 1826 rb-6-210

Baird, W. D. 1860 rb-20-699

Baird, William D. 1859 rb-20-203

Baird, Lemuel M. 1851 rb-16-116

Baird, William D. 1843 rb-12-345

Baker, Cynthia G. 1838 rb-10-194

Baker, Nathan 1824 rb-6-59

Baker, William 1807 rb-2-30

Balentine, Lemuel 1829 rb-7-176

Baley, William 1835 rb-9-201

Ballard, Wiley 1854 rb-17-162

Ballon, John B. 1859 rb-20-48

Banton, Lewis 1824 rb-6-30

Barber, John 1834 rb-9-144

Barkesdale, Nathaniel 1831 rb-8-329

Barkley, John 1850 rb-15-416

Barksdale, Nathaniel 1831 rb-8-254

Barksdale, Randolph 1844 rb-12-590

Barksdale, William 1834 rb-9-212

Barlow, Howard 1839 rb-10-307

Barnes, George A. 1858 rb-19-403

Barnes, James 1861 rb-20-756

Barnes, V. B. 1860 rb-20-597

Barnet, Jarret 1822 rb-5-251

Barns, Valuntine 1860 rb-20-466

Barr, Isaac 1804 rb-2-7

Barratt, Randolph 1857 rb-19-26

Barrett, Randol 1854 rb-17-185

Barry, James L. 1856 rb-18-189

Barton, David 1833 rb-9-22

Barton, Deubart? 1817 rb-4-27

Barton, Elizabeth 1860 rb-20-699

Barton, Howard 1841 rb-11-144

Barton, Isaac H. 1844 rb-12-431

Barton, Jesse 1839 rb-10-441

Barton, Rutha 1859 rb-20-35

Barton, Swinfield 1854 rb-17-159

Barton, Swinfield 1857 rb-18-367

Barton, Thomas 1817 rb-4-47

Barton, Thomas 1833 rb-9-17

Barton, David 1815 rb-3-47

Bass, Sarah 1829 rb-8-125

Bass, Uriah? 1829 rb-8-102

Bass, Heartuele 1826 rb-7-83

Bass, James sr. 1826 rb-6-219

Batey, James M. 1856 rb-18-163

Batey, W. D. 1858 rb-19-382

Batey, William 1835 rb-9-239

Batey, William D. 1858 rb-19-436

Batey, William F. 1850 rb-15-492

Batey, Christopher T. 1849 rb-15-49

Batey, James 1835 rb-9-213

Batey, James 1856 rb-18-156

Batin, Money 1835 rb-9-213

Batte, Viola 1840 rb-10-479

Batten, Nancy 1838 rb-10-141

Batton, Henry 1839 rb-10-249

Batton, John B. 1859 rb-19-568

Baty, Ann 1854 rb-17-210

Baty, D. W. 1859 rb-20-4

Baty, Rowlen 1817 rb-4-70

Bauton, Lewis 1826 rb-6-267

Baxter, David 1828 rb-7-195

Beasley, E. E. (Mrs) 1854 rb-16-783

Beasley, Eliza E. 1853 rb-16-648

Beasley, John W. 1850 rb-15-561

Beasley, Thomas 1828 rb-7-313

Beasly, Eliza E. 1856 rb-18-22

Beasly, Thomas 1838 rb-10-112

Beaty, Rowlin 1826 rb-6-222

Beaty, Wm. D. 1860 rb-20-640

Beaty, Wm. F. 1851 rb-16-69

Beavers, David C. 1849 rb-15-18

Beckton, George W. 1853 rb-16-467

Bedford, Robert 1860 rb-20-692

Bedford, Thomas 1805 rb-1-23

Bedford, Robert 1813 rb-3-111

Beesley, Major P. 1847 rb-14-80

Beesley, Thomas 1828 rb-7-153

Beesley, William 1846 rb-13-711

Beesley, John 1819 rb-4-185

Beeton, G. W. 1855 rb-17-428

Beevers, Abraham 1845 rb-13-411

Bell, James 1851 rb-15-618

Bell, James W. 1858 rb-19-435

Bell, Joseph 1853 rb-16-664

Bell, Joseph C. 1850 rb-15-438

Bell, Joseph W. 1860 rb-20-643

Bell, Zachariah P. 1824 rb-6-73

Bell, James 1828 rb-7-93

Bell, John 1854 rb-17-187

Bell, Sarah E. 1860 rb-20-637

Bellah, Moses 1828 rb-7-117

Bellah, Samuel 1832 rb-8-497

Bellah, Moses 1828 rb-7-295

Belt, Benjamin 1837 rb-10-539

Benson, William B. 1837 rb-10-59

Benson, Wm. W. 1835 rb-9-212

Berge, Nathaniel 1844 rb-13-15

Berry, James 1826 rb-6-193

Berry, James 1854 rb-17-116

Berry, James L. 1857 rb-18-407

Berry, James 1814 rb-3-107

Bethell, Isaac C. 1861 rb-21-93

Bethshares, William 1849 rb-15-47

Bethshares, William H. 1847 rb-14-78

Bethshares, William S. 1847 rb-14-95

Bethshears, Thomas 1859 rb-19-570

Biles (Boiles?), Obediah 1850 rb-15-439

Biles, John 1822 rb-5-197

Bill, Joseph W. 1858 rb-19-402

Bingham, William 1843 rb-12-387

Birthright, Samuel 1832 rb-9-10

Birthright, Lemuel 1832 rb-8-423

Bivins, Fielder 1844 rb-13-36

Bivins, James 1859 rb-20-128

Bivins, Jesse A. 1854 rb-17-322

Black, James A. 1835 rb-9-250

Black, Lucy A. (Miss) 1851 rb-16-97

Black, Lucy A. 1851 rb-15-567

Black, Mary 1816 rb-3-210
Black, Saml. P. 1837 rb-10-56
Black, Samuel 1838 rb-10-99
Black, Thomas 1816 rb-3-203
Blackman, A. J. 1858 rb-19-437
Blackman, James A. 1858 rb-19-480
Blackman, Lazarus 1852 rb-16-322
Blackman, Ollen M. 1840 rb-11-50
Blackman, Polly 1827 rb-6-317
Blackwood, James sr. 1852 rb-16-344
Blackwood, James 1850 rb-15-448
Blair, Richey 1856 rb-17-609
Blakely, James H. 1830 rb-8-66
Blakemore, William 1818 rb-4-145
Blanks, Ingram 1825 rb-6-174
Blanton, Celia 1853 rb-16-465
Blanton, Nelson 1820 rb-5-63
Blanton, Scilly 1854 rb-17-245
Blanton, Thomas 1846 rb-13-606
Blanton, John F. 1833 rb-9-64
Bolles, Nancy 1845 rb-13-64
Bolton, Asa 1851 rb-15-567
Bond, Solomon 1853 rb-16-464
Bonds, Daniel B. 1861 rb-21-49
Bone, Amos M. 1850 rb-15-235
Bone, William L. 1849 rb-15-162
Booker, Richard 1827 rb-7-105
Booker, Richardson 1827 rb-7-287
Boon, Simeon 1847 rb-14-64
Boone, Simeon W. 1847 rb-14-94
Booth, George C. 1844 rb-12-587
Boring, Amon 1839 rb-10-310
Boring, Martha L. 1854 rb-17-324
Boring, Nancy 1841 rb-11-318
Bostick, M. M. 1859 rb-19-624
Bowman, Daniel 1861 rb-21-149
Bowman, David 1839 rb-10-368
Bowman, James F. 1855 rb-17-413
Bowman, James T. 1855 rb-17-468
Bowman, Joseph 1831 rb-8-362
Bowman, Saml. (Maj.) 1838 rb-10-153
Bowman, Saml. 1855 rb-17-516
Bowman, Daniel 1844 rb-12-431
Bowman, John 1827 rb-7-343
Bowman, Joseph 1818 rb-4-181
Bowman, Samuel sr. 1838 rb-10-102

Boyd, Joel 1828 rb-7-187
Bradford, Eli M. 1838 rb-10-201
Bradford, James 1849 rb-15-6
Bradley, Hetty 1859 rb-19-528
Bradley, John 1853 rb-16-565
Brady, Susan C. 1859 rb-20-152
Brady, William J. 1830 rb-8-405
Brady, Wm. 1851 rb-16-504
Bragg, Thomas 1836 rb-9-296
Brandon, George 1844 rb-12-555
Brashear, Jesse 1822 rb-5-253
Brawly (Braley), Hugh Press? 1811 rb-2-165
Brewer, Martha 1853 rb-16-466
Briggs, Sarah (Mrs) 1854 rb-17-266
Briggs, Sarah 1853 rb-16-594
Brittain, John 1859 rb-20-193
Broiles, Alfred 1831 rb-8-297
Broiles, Elizabeth 1850 rb-15-300
Broils, Elijah 1852 rb-16-221
Broils, Matthias 1818 rb-4-113
Broils, Matthias 1842 rb-12-176
Brookshire, James 1813 rb-2-228
Brothers, Frances 1856 rb-18-122
Brothers, John 1847 rb-14-181
Brothers, John F. 1847 rb-14-65
Brothers, Thomas 1850 rb-15-440
Brothers, Francis 1845 rb-13-218
Brothers, John 1825 rb-6-110
Brown, John 1851 rb-15-600
Brown, Philip J. 1849 rb-15-118
Brown, Robert 1855 rb-17-495
Brown, Thomas 1860 rb-20-590
Brown, William 1827 rb-6-290
Brown, William F. 1843 rb-12-297
Brown, Isaac C. 1839 rb-10-271
Brown, John sr. 1849 rb-15-4
Brown, Lent 1851 rb-16-136
Browning, Elias 1809 rb-2-80
Bryan, James 1853 rb-16-709
Bryant, James H. 1856 rb-17-686
Buchanan, Charles B. 1836 rb-9-325
Buckner, William 1811 rb-2-113
Bugg, Benjamin 1811 rb-2-146
Bugg, Benjamin 1847 rb-14-171
Bumpass, Ann E. 1844 rb-12-430
Bumpass, R. W. 1858 rb-19-491

Bumpass, Robert 1845 rb-13-153

Bumpass, Robert W. 1858 rb-19-517

Burge, Alfred A. 1844 rb-12-564

Burge, Nathaniel J. 1844 rb-12-564

Burgess, Edward 1840 rb-11-81

Burks, Robert L. 1848 rb-14-424

Burlason, David 1832 rb-8-499

Burlerson, Ursula 1835 rb-9-226

Burnett, Brooking 1836 rb-9-311

Burnett, Edmond 1806 rb-2-10

Burnett, James 1851 rb-15-617

Burnett, Martha 1831 rb-8-320

Burnett, Nancy 1837 rb-9-416

Burnett, Reuben 1835 rb-9-227

Burnett, Sarah 1858 rb-19-403

Burnett, Henry 1838 rb-10-183

Burnett, Mathew 1831 rb-8-192

Burnett, William 1845 rb-13-225

Burns, Tarrance 1815 rb-3-31

Burrus, Fayett 1854 rb-17-313

Burrus, Joseph 1834 rb-9-151

Burrus, Lafayett 1856 rb-18-241

Burrus, Lucy 1825 rb-6-104

Burrus, S. 1835 rb-9-253

Burrus, W. C. J. 1859 rb-20-183

Burrus, W. J. 1859 rb-20-81

Burrus, Joseph 1821 rb-5-100

Burt, William H. 1856 rb-17-617

Burton, Ruth 1857 rb-18-389

Burton, Hardy M. 1853 rb-16-433

Butler, Elias 1821 rb-5-114

Butler, Isaac 1830 rb-8-9

Butler, Ann 1828 rb-7-306

Buttler, William 1838 rb-10-77

Butts, Benj. 1833 rb-9-29

Butts, Benjamin C. 1834 rb-9-121

Butts, Francis 1851 rb-16-108

Byler, Abraham 1846 rb-13-463

Cain, George I. 1837 rb-10-9

Cain, George J. 1853 rb-16-674

Cain, George L. 1853 rb-16-710

Cain, Martha M. 1853 rb-16-675

Cain, George J. 1834 rb-9-209

Cain, Martha Mary 1842 rb-12-145

Calhoun, George 1842 rb-12-257

Calvett, John 1816 rb-3-130

Campbell, Samuel 1846 rb-13-709

Cannon, Abram 1832 rb-9-7

Cannon, John M. 1839 rb-10-355

Cannon, Theopholus 1838 rb-10-148

Cannon, James R. 1843 rb-12-383

Cannon, John M. 1839 rb-10-360

Cannon, Joseph 1857 rb-19-65

Cannon, Joseph F. 1841 rb-12-53

Cannon, Theophilus A. 1836 rb-9-291

Canon, Jemima 1849 rb-15-216

Canon, Jemima A. 1849 rb-15-141

Carlton, Benajah 1850 rb-15-455

Carlton, Blake 1856 rb-18-158

Carmichael, Alexander 1820 rb-5-59

Carnahan, Andrew 1853 rb-16-413

Carnahan, Sarah 1859 rb-20-204

Carnahan, Andrew 1839 rb-10-358

Carney, Robartes 1818 rb-4-180

Carter, James 1826 rb-6-184

Carter, John 1821 rb-5-153

Carter, Rady 1859 rb-20-153

Carter, Rhoda 1859 rb-20-277

Carter, Burrell 1823 rb-5-314

Carter, John 1824 rb-6-3

Carter, Sarah 1827 rb-6-316

Cartwright, Edward 1860 rb-20-520

Caruthers, Edmund 1827 rb-7-2

Cary, James 1848 rb-14-247

Casens, Louis 1859 rb-20-47

Cason, John 1806 rb-2-18

Castleman, Arthur L. 1850 rb-15-557

Caswell, Richard W. 1811 rb-2-136

Caswell, Richard W. 1826 rb-6-213

Cates, Eliza 1846 rb-13-715

Cates, John 1848 rb-14-486

Cates, Joshua 1838 rb-10-216

Cates, Nancy 1857 rb-18-389

Cavit, John 1818 rb-4-111

Chalders, R. B. 1854 rb-17-30

Chandler, R. B. 1854 rb-17-48

Chandler, Robert B. 1856 rb-18-29

Cheatham, Thomas 1834 rb-9-90

Cheatham, Paulinia 1835 rb-9-195

Childress, George 1845 rb-13-385

Childress, Joel 1820 rb-4-192

Childs, Lois 1848 rb-14-389

Chisenall, John 1846 rb-13-542

Chisenhall, John 1825 rb-6-149

Chism, Edmund 1847 rb-14-4

Clardy, Thomas 1830 rb-8-148

Clark, Abigail 1854 rb-16-688

Clark, Abigail H. 1851 rb-16-120

Clark, E. T. 1858 rb-19-150

Clark, E. Y. 1855 rb-17-526

Clark, Elenor 1843 rb-12-416

Clark, Erastus Y. 1858 rb-19-203

Clark, James 1842 rb-12-82

Clark, John 1829 rb-7-167

Clark, John 1842 rb-12-238

Clark, Mary 1838 rb-10-124

Clark, Anthony 1827 rb-7-333

Clark, John 1857 rb-19-13

Claud, Francis 1851 rb-16-141

Claud, Francis M. 1849 rb-15-185

Clay, Armstead 1841 rb-11-241

Clay, Dennis 1818 rb-4-174

Clay, John 1837 rb-10-36

Cock, Wm. 1835 rb-9-230

Cock, Nancy 1842 rb-12-227

Cole, Thomas 1847 rb-14-172

Cole, Thomas H. 1855 rb-17-582

Coleman, John 1838 rb-10-169

Coleman, Sarah 1845 rb-13-170

Coleman, Sarah G. 1845 rb-13-115

Coleman, William A. 1849 rb-15-144

Coleman, Wyott 1839 rb-10-402

Coleman, Richard 1841 rb-11-286

Coleman, William 1846 rb-13-690

Coleman, William sr. 1842 rb-13-117

Colin, Mary C. 1830 rb-8-82

Collier, J. B. 1842 rb-12-105

Collier, Ingram B. 1842 rb-12-116

Comer, Adam 1859 rb-20-303

Comer, George 1850 rb-15-376

Conly, Thomas K. 1840 rb-11-80

Cook, Anderson 1843 rb-12-384

Cook, John S. 1837 rb-10-80

Cook, Mary 1860 rb-20-592

Cook, Anderson 1843 rb-12-388

Cook, Charlott S. 1852 rb-16-346

Cook, Green 1840 rb-10-489

Cooke, John D. 1854 rb-17-178

Cooper, Benjamin 1820 rb-4-223

Cooper, William B. 1848 rb-14-362

Cooper, Robert 1833 rb-9-61

Corbell, Thomas 1815 rb-3-62

Corner, George 1847 rb-14-172

Cosby, Hartwell 1838 rb-10-109

Cosby, Mary A. 1840 rb-10-553

Cotter, William 1828 rb-7-49

Cotter, Catharine 1830 rb-8-151

Cousins, Lewis 1859 rb-19-625

Covington, David 1840 rb-11-102

Covington, Lafayette 1857 rb-18-298

Covington, M. L. 1847 rb-14-17

Covington, M. P. 1857 rb-18-296

Covington, David 1830 rb-8-131

Covington, John 1847 rb-14-39

Coward, David 1820 rb-5-19

Cox, Elijah 1840 rb-10-477

Cox, John F. 1844 rb-12-574

Cox, Jonathan 1814 rb-2-306

Cox, Elijah 1840 rb-10-480

Cox, William 1836 rb-9-189

Cradock, John 1846 rb-13-688

Craig, John 1814 rb-2-279

Crawford, James 1860 rb-20-413

Crawford, Charles B. 1845 rb-13-177

Crawford, John 1843 rb-12-306

Crawford, Lazarus 1818 rb-4-164

Crawley, Lemuel 1840 rb-10-556

Crichloe, Thomas H. 1856 rb-17-610

Crocker, John T. 1840 rb-11-32

Crockett, Fountain P. 1838 rb-10-90

Crockett, P. P? 1837 rb-9-457

Crockett, Wm. M. 1856 rb-18-97

Cross, John 1835 rb-9-267

Crossthwait, Thomas 1816 rb-3-101

Crostwait, Shelton 1826 rb-6-223

Crouse, Mathius 1831 rb-8-403

Crouse, Spencer 1860 rb-20-591

Crowley, Lemuel 1840 rb-10-552

Crutchfield, Sarah 1827 rb-7-100

Cummins, John 1804 rb-2-1

Cummins, Richard W. 1838 rb-10-130

Cunningham, William 1843 rb-12-312

Curd, John 1837 rb-10-61

Curle, John 1812 rb-2-210

Currie, Mary (Mrs) 1835 rb-9-226

Currin, Jonathan 1843 rb-12-412

Dameron, Phebia 1851 rb-15-568

Dameron, Tegner 1824 rb-6-54

Dameron, Tigner 1824 rb-6-57

Daniel, Alexander 1857 rb-19-71

Daniel, Jeabud 1856 rb-17-691

Daniel, Mary E. 1847 rb-14-174

Daniel, Teabud 1854 rb-17-2

Daniel, J. P. 1858 rb-19-320

Dannel, Eden 1828 rb-7-190

Dansey, William 1818 rb-4-157

Dansy? (Dasy?), William S. 1814 rb-1-165

Dausy, William 1812 rb-2-265

Davidson, James 1816 rb-3-122

Davidson, John 1822 rb-5-185

Davis, Charles 1826 rb-6-223

Davis, Elizabeth 1854 rb-17-160

Davis, Elizabeth jr. 1812 rb-2-200

Davis, Elizabeth sr. 1812 rb-2-210

Davis, Ira P. 1848 rb-14-435

Davis, James 1842 rb-12-166

Davis, James M. 1842 rb-12-83

Davis, John 1820 rb-4-215

Davis, John 1830 rb-8-90

Davis, Lewis 1854 rb-17-158

Davis, Nancy 1840 rb-11-81

Davis, Samuel H. 1854 rb-17-323

Davis, William 1836 rb-9-297

Davis, Wm. H. 1852 rb-16-323

Davis, Wm. L. 1838 rb-10-173

Davis, Babby 1847 rb-14-40

Davis, Elizabeth 1809 rb-2-85

Davis, Lewis 1834 rb-9-218

Davis, Luckett sr. 1844 rb-13-2

Deckie, William 1860 rb-20-467

Deen, Richard 1831 rb-8-400

Deens, Richard 1831 rb-8-265

Dejarnett, Daniel 1858 rb-20-20

Dejarnett, Daniel M. 1858 rb-19-426

Dejarnett, James 1847 rb-14-189

Dejarnett, James 1834 rb-9-143

Delbridge, Edward W. 1827 rb-6-326

Delbridge, Turner 1844 rb-12-434

Dement, Abner 1825 rb-6-127

Dement, Abner 1835 rb-9-209

Dement, C. 1861 rb-20-745

Dement, Edmond P. 1844 rb-12-568

Dement, Edward 1844 rb-12-434

Dement, Edward T. 1846 rb-13-540

Dement, Francis 1850 rb-15-557

Dement, George W. 1856 rb-18-191

Dement, Lesenby 1854 rb-16-713

Dement, Mary (Nancy) 1856 rb-18-190

Dement, Nancy (Mrs) 1859 rb-20-206

Dement, Cader 1849 rb-15-156

Dement, Mary 1854 rb-17-270

Denney, Robert 1848 rb-14-324

Dickenson, Thomas J. 1847 rb-14-8

Dickie, William 1860 rb-20-463

Dickinson, Barbary 1845 rb-13-419

Dickinson, David W. 1845 rb-13-177

Dickinson, Sarah 1846 rb-13-531

Dickinson, Thomas J. 1844 rb-13-11

Dickinson, William 1860 rb-20-465

Dickinson, David 1848 rb-14-411

Dickinson, William 1816 rb-3-97

Dickson, Enoch 1841 rb-11-148

Dickson, Enos H. 1841 rb-11-105

Dickson, James 1844 rb-12-573

Dickson, Janah (Mrs) 1844 rb-12-477

Dickson, Joseph (Genl.) 1825 rb-6-143

Dickson, Enoch 1841 rb-11-151

Dickson, Enos H. 1841 rb-11-111

Dickson, Francis 1851 rb-15-589

Dickson, John 1823 rb-5-258

Dickson, Joseph 1825 rb-6-114

Dickson, Polly 1828 rb-7-305

Dickson, Thomas sr. 1828 rb-7-300

Dickson, William 1837 rb-9-407

Dill, Gilly 1854 rb-17-321

Dill, Isaac 1857 rb-18-266

Dill, Newton C. 1855 rb-17-495

Dill, William 1847 rb-14-164

Dill, Isaac 1846 rb-13-535

Dill, Joseph 1826 rb-6-255

Dill, William C. 1847 rb-14-135

Dillard, Martha 1838 rb-10-171

Dillon, John 1843 rb-12-405

Doak, John sr. 1828 rb-7-201

Doak, Margaret 1831 rb-8-212

Doak, John sr. 1828 rb-7-321

Dobbin, John 1857 rb-18-588

Dobbins, Andrew 1849 rb-15-206

Dobrowskie, P. M. 1861 rb-21-94

Dodd, Griffen 1840 rb-11-82

Dodd, Margaret 1858 rb-19-227

Dodd, Griffen 1840 rb-11-85

Dodd, Peggy 1858 rb-19-222

Donall, Thos. 1854 rb-16-773

Donelson, Jacob D. 1853 rb-16-711

Donelson, Lemuel 1842 rb-12-252

Donnel, Edin 1828 rb-7-289

Donnel, Elizabeth 1834 rb-9-118

Donnell, Thos. 1853 rb-16-671

Donnell, Robert S. 1847 rb-14-1

Donnell, Thos. 1854 rb-16-703

Donoho, Edward 1827 rb-7-136

Donoho, Robert 1838 rb-10-161

Donoho, William 1856 rb-18-96

Donoho, Robt. D. 1836 rb-9-337

Doran, Mary 1839 rb-10-381

Doran, William 1834 rb-9-220

Doran, William 1835 rb-9-161

Douglas, Luke 1821 rb-5-129

Dovicy, William 1813 rb-2-209

Dun, Richard 1834 rb-9-94

Dunaway, Samuel 1817 rb-4-93

Dunaway, Samuel 1851 rb-15-631

Dunaway, Thomas 1861 rb-20-782

Duncan, Rachael 1845 rb-13-116

Duncan, Marshall 1833 rb-9-64

Dunn, Henry F. 1838 rb-10-115

Dunn, Henry T. 1836 rb-9-304

Dunn, John 1835 rb-9-222

Dunn, Thomas D. 1851 rb-15-586

Dunn, William A. 1839 rb-10-357

Dunnaway, Nancy 1855 rb-17-586

Dyer, Isaiah 1857 rb-18-390

Dyer, Josiah 1859 rb-19-607

Early, Caleb 1853 rb-16-707

Earthman, Jas. 1835 rb-9-199

Eaton, Isaac 1813 rb-2-243

Eaton, Nathan 1828 rb-7-43

Eaton, Joseph H. 1859 rb-19-566

Edwards, Arther M. 1854 rb-17-275

Edwards, John W. 1847 rb-14-204

Edwards, Thomas M. 1852 rb-16-320

Edwards, William 1824 rb-6-53

Edwards, Matthew 1821 rb-5-61

Edwards, Owen 1821 rb-5-90

Edwards, Thomas 1850 rb-15-236

Elam, Daniel 1829 rb-7-168

Elam, Daniel 1829 rb-7-308

Elder, James 1824 rb-6-67

Elgin, Saml. 1849 rb-15-186

Elliott, Catharine 1839 rb-10-462

Elliott, Hiram 1861 rb-21-48

Elliott, Nacy 1849 rb-15-61

Elliott, Richard R. 1859 rb-19-528

Elliott, Samuel J. 1859 rb-19-527

Elliott, Deborah 1829 rb-7-303

Elliott, James 1836 rb-9-390

Elliott, William 1835 rb-9-248

Ellis, Hicks 1860 rb-20-339

Ellis, Sophia B. 1859 rb-20-187

Ellis, W. A. 1855 rb-17-450

Ellis, William 1837 rb-9-409

Ellis, Wyott H. 1847 rb-14-5

Ellis, Hicks 1860 rb-20-344

Elrod, Jeremiah 1841 rb-12-45

Elrod, Jeremiah 1841 rb-12-74

Endaley, Jas. 1831 rb-8-214

Epps, Rebecca 1856 rb-18-235

Epps, Edward 1813 rb-2-226

Erasly?, Thomas 1820 rb-4-263

Espey, James 1813 rb-2-235

Espy, Robert A. 1858 rb-19-223

Ethridge, Bassett 1824 rb-6-23

Etter, John 1851 rb-15-585

Evans, Ezekiel 1855 rb-17-494

Evans, George 1830 rb-8-64

Evans, James D. 1841 rb-12-52

Evans, John 1844 rb-13-42

Evans, Nancy 1858 rb-19-401

Evans, David 1843 rb-12-416

Evans, Thomas 1820 rb-4-209

Evens, L. J. 1829 rb-7-229

Fagan, Henry 1855 rb-17-579

Fagan, Henry W. 1855 rb-17-525

Fagans, John 1820 rb-5-58

Fagg, Charles 1826 rb-6-218

Fan, Elijah 1813 rb-2-249

Farmer, Bailey W. 1850 rb-15-491

Farmer, Enoch 1858 rb-19-219

Farmer, Enoch J. 1858 rb-19-155

Farmer, Joseph A. 1839 rb-10-430

Farmer, Thomas 1835 rb-9-250

Farr, Ephraim 1842 rb-12-84

Farr, Ephraim 1842 rb-12-86

Fathera, J. C. 1858 rb-19-355

Faucett, James L. 1857 rb-18-437

Faucett, James S. 1857 rb-18-391

Faulkenberry, David 1841 rb-12-30

Featherston, Presley 1816 rb-3-216

Feerr?, George 1828 rb-7-9

Ferguson, John 1833 rb-9-85

Ferris, Mary J. 1859 rb-20-154

Ferriss, Josiah 1842 rb-12-278

Ferriss, Josiah sr. 1841 rb-11-109

Field, John 1853 rb-16-436

Fields, Elizabeth 1859 rb-20-276

Fields, Winney 1817 rb-4-17

Finch, A. 1859 rb-20-242

Finch, Adam 1859 rb-20-320

Finch, John 1827 rb-7-77

Finch, John W. 1830 rb-8-75

Finch, Sarah 1853 rb-16-709

Finney, Andrew 1835 rb-9-198

Finney, Andrew 1845 rb-13-76

Finney, William 1854 rb-17-211

Finney, William 1854 rb-17-225

Fisher, Jno. 1820 rb-4-216

Fleman, Jacob 1831 rb-8-269

Fleming, Andrew 1849 rb-15-53

Fleming, J. M. 1859 rb-20-129

Fleming, Andrew J. 1849 rb-14-520

Flemming, David 1815 rb-3-10

Fletcher, Ann 1852 rb-16-342

Fletcher, Jeremiah W. 1842 rb-12-83

Fletcher, M. H. 1835 rb-9-260

Fletcher, Mary J. 1847 rb-14-78

Fletcher, Mary Jane 1847 rb-14-271

Fletcher, Mouthford H. 1836 rb-9-351

Fletcher, John 1849 rb-15-110

Flowers, Joseph 1849 rb-15-118

Floyd, Rebecca 1849 rb-15-109

Floyd, Richd. J. 1853 rb-16-566

Flyn, Cornelius O. 1825 rb-6-172

Flynn, Cornelius O. 1860 rb-20-640

Fogg, Charles 1822 rb-5-248

Ford, Joshua 1844 rb-12-500

Ford, Judith 1840 rb-10-479

Ford, Nathan 1828 rb-7-200

Ford, Nathan 1845 rb-13-150

Ford, John 1809 rb-1-72

Ford, John 1809 rb-2-65

Forknor, Henrietta 1846 rb-13-712

Fosset, John 1835 rb-9-187

Foster, Richard 1825 rb-6-127

Foster, Sarah 1855 rb-17-531

Foster, William 1827 rb-7-109

Foster, William 1828 rb-7-315

Fowler, William 1830 rb-8-129

Fox, Elizabeth 1850 rb-15-415

Fox, Jacob 1831 rb-8-175

Fox, Jacob 1844 rb-13-75

Freeman (B), Andrew 1839 rb-10-337

Freeman, Andrew 1825 rb-6-132

Freeman, James 1811 rb-2-153

Freeman, Robert 1831 rb-8-169

Freeman, Andrew 1825 rb-6-121

Freeman, Asa 1861 rb-21-128

Frost, Thomas 1806 rb-2-11

Fulk, Samuel 1860 rb-20-623

Fulks, John 1845 rb-13-178

Fulks, John D. 1843 rb-12-311

Fulks, Samuel 1845 rb-13-387

Fulks, Samuel 1860 rb-20-622

Fulks, William 1848 rb-14-320

Fulks, John 1856 rb-18-159

Fuller, Arthur 1815 rb-3-83

Fuller, Susan 1846 rb-13-689

Fuller, John 1852 rb-16-148

Fuller, Levi 1837 rb-10-7

Furr, George 1830 rb-8-41

Fussell, Harrison 1829 rb-7-217

Fuzell, John 1839 rb-10-455

Gable, William 1818 rb-4-107

Gainer, Obadiah 1824 rb-6-50

Gaither, Brice 1828 rb-7-132

Gaither, Brice M. 1831 rb-8-183

Gambell, John K. 1845 rb-13-163

Gambill, Bradley 1806 rb-2-21

Gambill, John 1843 rb-12-380

Gambril, John R. 1854 rb-17-279

Gammill, Samuel 1817 rb-4-80
Gannaway, Elijah R. 1852 rb-16-335
Gannaway, Burrel 1853 rb-16-646
Garaway, Robt. 1812 rb-2-203
Garaway, John 1812 rb-2-204
Gardner, Uriah 1830 rb-8-83
Gardner, Uriah 1830 rb-8-96
Garner, John 1817 rb-4-96
Garner, John N. 1847 rb-14-170
Garner, Obadiah 1822 rb-5-176
Garratt, Henry 1859 rb-20-82
Garrison, Peter 1824 rb-6-44
Gasaway, John 1813 rb-2-216
Gasaway, Robert 1814 rb-3-15
Gates, Wm. 1847 rb-14-226
Gates, Wm. M. 1846 rb-13-693
Gatewood, Sarah 1853 rb-16-466
Gather, Brice 1830 rb-8-146
Gather, Buie 1828 rb-7-119
Gatlin, Mary 1824 rb-6-42
Gibson, Joseph 1815 rb-3-171
Gibson, James 1835 rb-9-258
Gilleland, James 1815 rb-3-6
Gillespey, James 1859 rb-20-146
Gillespie, Mary 1831 rb-8-402
Gillespie, James 1857 rb-18-499
Gilliam, William 1842 rb-12-107
Gilliam, William 1860 rb-20-686
Gilliam, Harrison 1808 rb-2-60
Gilliam, Isham 1848 rb-14-251
Gilliam, Richard 1842 rb-12-195
Gilmore, Peter 1858 rb-19-293
Gilmore, William 1837 rb-10-2
Gleaves, Thomas 1841 rb-12-4
Glymph, James B. 1856 rb-17-614
Glympth, James 1856 rb-18-106
Gooch, John 1857 rb-18-359
Gooch, John C. 1854 rb-16-713
Gooch, Nathaniel 1841 rb-12-53
Gooch, Samuel 1857 rb-18-351
Gooch, Nathaniel 1841 rb-12-55
Good, Elizabeth 1834 rb-9-145
Good, Henry 1840 rb-10-508
Good, Henry 1855 rb-17-358
Good, Hugh 1845 rb-13-364
Good, James O. 1854 rb-17-273

Good, John 1834 rb-9-169
Good, John F. 1833 rb-9-46
Good, Mary 1834 rb-9-167
Good, Sarah 1845 rb-13-163
Good, Elizabeth 1836 rb-9-115
Good, John T. 1833 rb-9-15
Goodlett, Adam G. 1850 rb-15-412
Goodlett, A. G. 1850 rb-15-377
Goodloe, Henry 1846 rb-13-646
Goodloe, John 1830 rb-8-58
Goodloe, Rebecca 1852 rb-16-350
Goodloe, Thompson 1847 rb-14-173
Goodloe, Thompson W. 1849 rb-15-231
Goodloe, T. W. 1847 rb-14-173
Goodlow, Hannah 1857 rb-19-120
Goodman, Albert G. 1854 rb-17-159
Goodman, Alferd 1854 rb-17-328
Goodman, George 1833 rb-9-26
Goodman, William 1850 rb-15-502
Goodman, William sr. 1850 rb-15-438
Goodman, Edmund 1845 rb-13-216
Goodman, George 1815 rb-3-34
Goss, Elijah 1846 rb-13-714
Gowan, Alford P. 1857 rb-18-437
Gowen, James F. 1836 rb-9-336
Gowen, Harriet 1839 rb-10-432
Green, John 1828 rb-7-22
Green, John 1844 rb-13-1
Green, Thomas C. 1844 rb-12-563
Greene, Morris 1816 rb-3-191
Greenlee, Samuel 1849 rb-14-501
Greer, Nathan 1856 rb-18-182
Greer, John 1828 rb-7-307
Greer, Nathan 1856 rb-18-127
Gregory, Barbary 1840 rb-11-54
Gregory, Edward 1842 rb-12-105
Gregory, Frances 1842 rb-12-223
Gregory, Francis 1853 rb-16-576
Gregory, Edward 1842 rb-12-113
Gregory, Edwin 1836 rb-9-393
Gresham, Wm. A. 1861 rb-20-800
Griffen, James 1840 rb-11-21
Griffin, James 1853 rb-16-479
Griffin, Sarah 1853 rb-16-375
Griffin, Sarah C. 1850 rb-15-491
Grigg, Lewis 1836 rb-9-392

Grigory, Martha A. 1852 rb-16-240

Grisham, William 1836 rb-9-370

Grisham, William 1848 rb-14-365

Grogan, James H. 1850 rb-15-394

Gupton, Cooper 1819 rb-4-211

Guthrie, Wm. H. 1852 rb-16-323

Hager, William 1835 rb-9-251

Hale, William 1843 rb-17-100

Hall, Alfred G. 1846 rb-13-693

Hall, Andrew 1854 rb-17-209

Hall, Elizabeth 1855 rb-17-584

Hall, Jacob 1844 rb-12-527

Hall, John 1816 rb-3-187

Hall, John 1846 rb-13-692

Hall, John sr. 1854 rb-17-346

Hall, R. B. 1848 rb-14-399

Hall, Randolph 1848 rb-14-325

Hall, Randolph B. 1849 rb-15-232

Hall, W. M. 1830 rb-8-134

Hall, Andrew 1854 rb-17-226

Hall, Gideon B. 1861 rb-21-14

Hall, Jacob sr. 1844 rb-12-525

Hall, John 1853 rb-16-396

Hall, Thomas 1832 rb-8-500

Hallyburton, Richd. 1853 rb-16-565

Hallyburton, Susannah 1855 rb-17-526

Hallyburton, Susan 1855 rb-18-125

Hallyburton, William H. 1854 rb-17-188

Hamilton, Hance 1816 rb-3-186

Hamilton, Thomas 1834 rb-9-162

Hamilton, Thomas 1854 rb-16-706

Hamilton, Mary 1830 rb-8-152

Hampton, John 1818 rb-4-128

Hancock, Francis 1851 rb-16-44

Hancock, Thomas 1851 rb-15-619

Hankins, Wm. 1830 rb-8-145

Hanley, Crawford 1838 rb-10-91

Hanna, Samuel W. 1846 rb-13-465

Hardeman, Constantine 1850 rb-15-439

Hardeman, Mary 1859 rb-19-624

Hare, Bryant 1825 rb-6-123

Harney, George W. 1805 rb-2-8

Harrell, Henry 1851 rb-16-138

Harrell, Lewis 1853 rb-16-708

Harris, Beverly 1850 rb-15-370

Harris, Beverly sr. 1849 rb-14-500

Harris, James R. 1841 rb-12-6

Harris, Simpson 1833 rb-9-70

Harris, Simpson 1852 rb-16-322

Harris, Thomas A. 1828 rb-8-121

Harris, William G. 1819 rb-4-208

Harris, Alsea 1847 rb-14-196

Harris, Archibald 1823 rb-5-315

Harrison, D. A. 1857 rb-19-17

Harrison, James A. 1848 rb-14-370

Harrison, Joshua 1826 rb-6-261

Harrison, Sophia (Mrs) 1856 rb-17-719

Harrison, Dorothy 1840 rb-11-4

Harrison, Sophia 1855 rb-17-470

Hart, James F. 1845 rb-13-145

Hart, Mark 1846 rb-13-503

Hart, William G. 1858 rb-19-490

Hart, Mark 1835 rb-9-202

Hartless, William 1838 rb-10-200

Hartman, John 1844 rb-12-533

Hartwell, Armstead 1855 rb-17-469

Harwell, Littleberry S. 1821 rb-5-166

Hawley, Crawford 1838 rb-10-145

Hayes, Samuel 1815 rb-3-53

Hayes, Adam 1833 rb-9-16

Hayes, Archerbald 1845 rb-13-145

Haynes, James M. 1854 rb-17-64

Haynes, John S. 1852 rb-16-335

Haynes, John W. 1856 rb-18-161

Haynes, Margaret A. 1855 rb-17-527

Haynes, Nathaniel 1852 rb-16-319

Haynes, Abraham 1838 rb-10-195

Haynes, Andrew J. 1859 rb-20-78

Haynes, Philadelphia 1829 rb-7-277

Hays, Archer 1845 rb-13-205

Heard, Armstrong 1830 rb-8-107

Heartwell, Alfred 1835 rb-9-256

Heath, Richard 1852 rb-16-351

Hedgepatch, Jesse 1821 rb-5-163

Hedgpeth, John 1835 rb-9-263

Heiflen, William C.? 1818 rb-4-132

Heifler, William 1817 rb-4-92

Helton, Peter 1849 rb-15-117

Helton, Robert 1840 rb-11-23

Henderson, James 1815 rb-3-28

Henderson, James 1857 rb-18-474

Henderson, John 1860 rb-20-624

Henderson, John L. 1840 rb-11-32

Henderson, Margaret 1854 rb-17-301

Henderson, William 1823 rb-5-283

Henderson, Wm. 1835 rb-9-187

Henderson, John 1828 rb-8-4

Henderson, Logan 1847 rb-13-743

Henderson, Samuel 1821 rb-5-96

Hendrix, Catherine 1838 rb-10-130

Hendrix, Thomas 1857 rb-18-320

Henry, Rebecca L. 1861 rb-21-105

Herral, Mallissa J. 1859 rb-19-625

Herrald, Lewis 1856 rb-18-179

Herrall, Henry 1851 rb-15-631

Herrod, Henry 1851 rb-16-130

Heytton, Robert 1837 rb-10-58

Higgenbotham, Elijah 1851 rb-16-107

Higginbothom, John 1855 rb-17-585

Hill, James 1821 rb-5-160

Hill, William 1816 rb-3-125

Hind, James 1815 rb-3-117

Hodge, James 1835 rb-9-181

Hodge, James 1853 rb-16-669

Hodge, Samuel H. 1846 rb-13-531

Hodges, Mariah 1839 rb-10-410

Hogg, Samuel 1843 rb-12-307

Hogwood, Ransom 1827 rb-7-95

Holden, Charles 1861 rb-20-801

Holden, Dennis 1845 rb-13-225

Holden, William 1858 rb-19-353

Holloway, Isaac 1837 rb-10-10

Hollowell, J. R. B. 1856 rb-18-237

Hollowell, James J. 1850 rb-15-235

Hollowell, Robt. B. 1854 rb-17-273

Holmes, William 1826 rb-6-216

Holt, Micheal 1809 rb-2-75

Holt, Rebecca S. 1855 rb-17-360

Holton, Abel 1845 rb-13-412

Holton, Abel B. 1846 rb-13-515

Hood, Chesley 1829 rb-8-57

Hood, John H. 1856 rb-18-236

Hood, William H. 1859 rb-19-555

Hoods, W. H. 1857 rb-18-401

Hoover, A. J. 1838 rb-10-140

Hoover, Andrew J. 1847 rb-14-174

Hoover, Christopher 1844 rb-12-527

Hoover, Julius 1860 rb-20-401

Hoover, Martin 1840 rb-11-51

Hoover, Martin L. 1840 rb-11-89

Hoover, John 1845 rb-13-220

Horne, Simeon 1829 rb-7-208

Horne, Elizabeth 1828 rb-7-302

Hoskins, Daniel 1848 rb-14-249

Hoskins, Thomas C. 1839 rb-10-394*

House, Claiborne 1851 rb-16-111

House, John C. 1857 rb-18-455

Howell, Catharine F. 1854 rb-17-2

Howell, Francis 1854 rb-17-46

Howell, William 1814 rb-2-269

Howell, Gwin 1812 rb-3-109

Howell, John 1808 rb-2-49

Howse, Isaac L. 1841 rb-11-309

Howse, John C. 1855 rb-17-497

Howse, Keziah 1844 rb-13-129

Howse, Robert 1840 rb-11-260

Howse, Robert C. 1840 rb-11-54

Howse, Ambrose 1855 rb-17-498

Howse, Hezekiah 1844 rb-12-558

Howse, Isaac L. 1841 rb-11-313

Howse, John C. 1856 rb-17-786

Howse, Susan 1860 rb-20-415

Hubbard, John 1857 rb-18-276

Hudson, Enoch M. 1843 rb-12-419

Hudson, Henry M. 1823 rb-5-294

Huff, Wiley 1855 rb-17-412

Huggins, Elizabeth 1859 rb-19-570

Huggins, Robert D. 1836 rb-9-375

Hugh, Kirk 1851 rb-16-57

Hume, Jesse W. 1854 rb-17-274

Hunt, Christena 1841 rb-11-149

Hunt, James 1829 rb-7-167

Hunt, Mathew 1849 rb-15-232

Hunt, Nancy 1848 rb-14-220

Hunt, Matthew 1832 rb-8-421

Hust, Rebecca 1855 rb-17-469

Hutchenson, Sarah 1832 rb-8-467

Hutchinson, Thomas 1808 rb-2-71

Inglish, A. J. 1858 rb-19-381

Iseminger, William R. 1839 rb-10-267

Ivie, Sterling 1830 rb-8-62

Jackson, Anderson 1840 rb-11-26

Jackson, Francis 1845 rb-13-229

Jackson, Francis sr. 1845 rb-13-144

Jacobs, Allen 1850 rb-15-494

Jacobs, Alvin 1850 rb-15-441

Jacobs, Jackson 1847 rb-14-136

Jacobs, Jeremiah 1850 rb-15-487

Jacobs, John 1851 rb-16-138

Jacobs, Nancy 1861 rb-21-146

Jacobs, John 1852 rb-16-233

James, Cary 1848 rb-14-339

James, Doritha 1859 rb-20-47

James, Elizabeth 1846 rb-13-464

James, John P. 1841 rb-11-145

James, John P. sr. 1840 rb-11-83

James, Martha (Mrs) 1851 rb-16-74

James, Sarah 1818 rb-4-154

James, William 1852 rb-16-342

James, Allen 1851 rb-15-582

James, Anderson 1836 rb-9-93

James, Frances 1852 rb-16-289

James, John sr. 1840 rb-11-61

James, Martha 1851 rb-15-581

James, Mary 1846 rb-13-709

James, Thomas 1854 rb-17-238

Jameson, Samuel 1858 rb-19-490

Jamison, Henry D. 1859 rb-19-629

Jarman, Amous 1856 rb-18-186

Jarratt, Archibald 1832 rb-9-8

Jarratt, Joseph 1825 rb-6-103

Jarratt, Mary 1860 rb-20-528

Jarratt, Thomas 1855 rb-17-565

Jarratt, Thomas S. 1858 rb-19-153

Jarratt, Archilus 1831 rb-8-239

Jarratt, Rhoda 1852 rb-16-190

Jarratte, Thomas 1828 rb-7-37

Jenkins, Nimrod 1856 rb-17-614

Jenkins, Hiram 1857 rb-19-68

Jenkins, Nimrod 1837 rb-10-18

Jetton, Andrew 1843 rb-12-296

Jetton, Andrew J. 1843 rb-12-315

Jetton, Elizabeth 1852 rb-16-378

Jetton, James 1852 rb-16-258

Jetton, James M. 1849 rb-15-144

Jetton, Jas. S. 1851 rb-16-53

Jetton, John S. 1831 rb-8-199

Jetton, John S. 1858 rb-19-314

Jetton, John W. 1839 rb-10-267

Jetton, Mary S. 1850 rb-15-297

Jetton, Nancy 1855 rb-17-525

Jetton, Robert 1857 rb-18-352

Jetton, William 1850 rb-15-519

Jetton, William M. 1850 rb-15-415

Jetton, James L. 1850 rb-15-562

Jetton, John L. 1854 rb-17-182

Jetton, John White 1839 rb-10-276

Jetton, Robert 1841 rb-11-106

Jetton, Wilson B. F. 1845 rb-13-215

Johns, Ann 1813 rb-2-221

Johns, Edmund 1825 rb-6-162

Johns, Edward 1826 rb-6-288

Johns, Elizabeth 1844 rb-13-81

Johns, Franklin 1845 rb-13-248

Johns, Franklin A. 1845 rb-13-163

Johns, Isaac 1858 rb-19-402

Johns, John 1837 rb-9-412

Johns, Joseph B. 1839 rb-10-462

Johns, Joseph P. 1861 rb-21-148

Johns, Margaret W. 1849 rb-15-185

Johns, Mary 1820 rb-5-14

Johns, William R. 1830 rb-8-79

Johns, Abner 1825 rb-6-152

Johns, Edmund 1812 rb-2-158

Johns, Frederick 1843 rb-12-295

Johns, Jacob 1857 rb-19-117

Johnson, Archibald 1851 rb-16-137

Johnson, Benjamin 1848 rb-14-441

Johnson, Daniel H. 1857 rb-18-339

Johnson, Edward 1853 rb-16-403

Johnson, Edward M. 1849 rb-15-17

Johnson, Lewis jr. 1850 rb-15-455

Johnson, Lewis sr. 1853 rb-16-366

Johnson, Lucy 1857 rb-19-82

Johnson, Needham 1815 rb-3-62

Johnson, Oliver 1859 rb-20-241

Johnson, Philip 1831 rb-8-270

Johnson, Samuel 1859 rb-20-103

Johnson, Thomas 1837 rb-10-12

Johnson, Thomas 1847 rb-14-14

Johnson, William 1816 rb-3-126

Johnson, James 1828 rb-7-334

Johnson, Joshua 1839 rb-10-361

Johnson, William 1816 rb-3-147*

Johnston, David 1856 rb-18-162

Johnston, Lewis 1849 rb-15-186

Johnston, John 1825 rb-6-112

Johnston, Lewis 1849 rb-15-202

Jones, Anthony 1842 rb-12-253

Jones, Bedford 1848 rb-14-397

Jones, Bedford C. 1846 rb-13-689

Jones, David 1820 rb-5-20

Jones, Delilah 1855 rb-17-495

Jones, Elizabeth 1838 rb-10-189

Jones, Ezra 1839 rb-10-358

Jones, Ezra 1859 rb-20-140

Jones, James 1855 rb-17-530

Jones, James E. 1857 rb-18-637

Jones, Lewallen 1838 rb-10-92

Jones, Lucy 1847 rb-14-168

Jones, Nancy 1838 rb-10-214

Jones, Nathaniel 1821 rb-5-136

Jones, Richard 1835 rb-9-262

Jones, Willie 1815 rb-3-58

Jones, Anthony 1843 rb-12-312

Jones, Ezra 1839 rb-10-362

Jones, Henry 1847 rb-14-167

Jones, Patsy 1842 rb-12-200

Jones, Richard 1836 rb-9-203

Jones, William 1859 rb-19-627

Jordan, Blount 1851 rb-15-618

Jordan, J. B. 1859 rb-19-569

Jordan, James B. 1861 rb-21-6

Jordan, John 1850 rb-15-248

Jordan, John J. 1849 rb-15-78

Jordan, Nancy 1852 rb-16-236

Jordon, Alexander 1824 rb-6-63

Keas, David 1818 rb-4-121

Keeble, Eliza 1847 rb-14-64

Keeble, Jane C. 1857 rb-18-349

Keeble, Walter 1854 rb-16-786

Keeble, Walter 1844 rb-12-432

Keeble, Walter 1844 rb-13-50

Keebles, Walter 1816 rb-3-200

Keel, William 1861 rb-21-69

Keele, Richard 1833 rb-9-63

Keeling, Martha 1860 rb-20-464

Keer, Wilson 1827 rb-7-127

Keith, Danl. 1836 rb-9-126

Keller, Conrad 1821 rb-5-118

Kellough, Robert H. 1843 rb-12-350

Kellough, Samuel 1842 rb-12-123

Kelly, Saml. L. 1825 rb-6-124

Kelly, Stephen 1856 rb-17-718

Kelton, Robert 1829 rb-7-169

Kelton, Robert E. 1860 rb-20-621

Kelton, Samuel 1840 rb-11-80

Kelton, Samuel B. 1841 rb-11-222

Kelton, William 1813 rb-1-150

Kelton, William 1844 rb-13-43

Kelton, William R. 1844 rb-13-152

Kelton, Elizabeth 1830 rb-8-130

Kelton, James 1847 rb-14-168

Kenedy, Obediance 1848 rb-14-425

Kerby, George H. 1858 rb-19-219

Kerr, Wilson 1814 rb-1-166

Ketrell, Wm. 1834 rb-9-167

Kettrell, John 1838 rb-10-164

Keys, John 1816 rb-3-173

Kiellough, Samuel 1813 rb-2-215

Killough, John 1808 rb-2-60

Killough, Mary 1850 rb-15-301

Kimbro, Joseph 1860 rb-20-686

Kimbro, William 1816 rb-3-224

Kimbro, William 1833 rb-9-55

Kimbro, William G. 1839 rb-10-339

Kimbro, Wm. W. 1858 rb-19-142

Kimbro, W. W. 1853 rb-16-646

Kimbro, William G. 1825 rb-6-87

Kindrick, Thomas 1833 rb-9-62

King, Henry 1816 rb-3-181

King, John M. 1825 rb-6-141

King, Wm. R. 1852 rb-16-293

Kinnard, Michael 1813 rb-1-161

Kirk, Hugh 1850 rb-15-479

Kirk, James 1860 rb-21-39

Kirk, Jane 1860 rb-20-341

Kirk, Nancy M. 1847 rb-14-180

Kirk, John 1822 rb-5-250

Kitrell, John 1836 rb-9-339

Kitrell, Wilie 1833 rb-9-25

Knight, Eveline D. 1843 rb-12-351

Knight, John 1832 rb-8-420

Knox, Franklin 1856 rb-18-235

Knox, Joseph 1816 rb-3-170

Knox, Thomas 1821 rb-5-122

Knox, William 1814 rb-2-268

Knox, William F. 1854 rb-17-190

Knox, Joseph 1835 rb-9-257
Knox, Squire 1816 rb-3-132
Lackey, A. R. 1857 rb-18-557
Lackey, Alexr. 1853 rb-16-620
Lackey, W. K. 1858 rb-19-459
Lacky, Alexander R. 1857 rb-19-24
Lain, Noah 1854 rb-17-2
Lain, Noah W. 1854 rb-17-51
Lamb, David 1848 rb-14-325
Lambert, Jarvis 1846 rb-13-463
Lane, Benjamin 1846 rb-13-671
Lane, Benjamin W. 1844 rb-12-435
Lane, Caroline M. 1849 rb-15-145
Lane, Rebecca 1844 rb-13-10
Lane, Sally 1834 rb-9-187
Lanier, Lemuel 1817 rb-4-72
Lannam, William 1854 rb-17-186
Lannom, A. F. 1857 rb-18-537
Lannom, Artilla 1854 rb-17-274
Lannom, Levi L. 1857 rb-18-592
Lannom, William 1856 rb-18-124
Lannon, Levi 1849 rb-15-185
Lannum, Joseph 1823 rb-5-259
Lantern, Joseph 1841 rb-11-309
Lantern, Joseph 1841 rb-11-311
Lark, Dennis 1851 rb-15-623
Lasiter, Thomas 1839 rb-10-270
Laughlin, James Y. 1823 rb-6-12
Laughlin, Jane 1817 rb-4-83
Laughlin, Jean 1813 rb-2-241
Laughlin, John R. 1842 rb-12-118
Lawrance, John 1836 rb-9-324
Lawrence, Archerbald 1845 rb-13-416
Lawrence, Jane 1846 rb-13-715
Lawrence, Joanna (Mrs.) 1853 rb-17-255
Lawrence, Johanna 1853 rb-16-708
Lawrence, Jonathan 1826 rb-6-214
Lawrence, Joseph 1840 rb-11-79
Lawrence, Mary 1841 rb-12-26
Layne, Robert 1848 rb-14-370
Leathers, Anderson A. 1841 rb-12-20
Leavin?, P. H. 1815 rb-3-49
Ledbetter, Elenor C. 1838 rb-10-133
Ledbetter, David 1824 rb-6-61
Ledbetter, Isaac 1820 rb-5-52
Ledden, Benjamin 1814 rb-1-168

Ledon, Sarah 1838 rb-10-215
Lee, John 1828 rb-7-190
Leech, Thomas 1839 rb-10-311
Leek, John M. 1840 rb-11-55
Lenom, Thomas 1841 rb-11-148
Lenore, William N. 1859 rb-19-562
Lenster, Mary 1859 rb-20-77
Lewis, Benjamin 1844 rb-12-573
Lewis, Benjamin F. 1844 rb-13-23
Lewis, Elam 1840 rb-10-487
Lewis, Elam 1850 rb-15-556
Lewis, Gabriel 1852 rb-16-237
Lewis, Gabriel F. 1854 rb-17-32
Lewis, Mary 1855 rb-17-414
Lewis, Patsey (Martha) 1844 rb-12-498
Lewis, Samuel 1844 rb-12-501
Lewis, Joseph 1854 rb-16-787
Lewis, Martha (Patsey) 1844 rb-12-499
Lillard, Alexander 1847 rb-14-38
Lillard, Mordecia 1851 rb-16-134
Linam, Thomas 1840 rb-11-79
Linch, Elizabeth 1854 rb-17-17
Linch, John 1854 rb-17-16
Lindsey, Caleb 1839 rb-10-264
Lingo, Archibald 1859 rb-20-109
Linom, Elinor 1841 rb-11-191
Lisk, William 1858 rb-19-356
Lock, Sarah 1843 rb-12-311
Locke, William (Col.) 1833 rb-9-53
Locke, William 1832 rb-8-495
Loften, Lavinea 1826 rb-6-280
Loftin, Eldridge 1853 rb-16-566
Loftin, Mr. 1828 rb-7-44
Lofton, William 1811 rb-2-152
Lofton, William 1811 rb-2-184
Logan, Elizabeth 1848 rb-14-424
Long, Joseph 1857 rb-19-79
Long, Josiah 1858 rb-19-178
Love, Hugh 1846 rb-13-605
Love, Charles 1840 rb-11-63
Lovel, Markum 1846 rb-13-708
Loven, William 1849 rb-15-206
Lowe, Charles 1834 rb-9-198
Lowe, Henrietta 1832 rb-9-13
Lowe, John S. 1838 rb-10-155
Lowe, Mary 1848 rb-14-241

Lowe, Mary C. (Mrs.) 1861 rb-21-72

Lowe, Robert W. 1858 rb-19-382

Lowe, Walter 1827 rb-6-293

Lowe, Walter 1839 rb-10-410

Lowe, Walter S. 1844 rb-12-501

Lowe, Charles 1836 rb-9-326

Lowe, Mary C. 1860 rb-20-386

Lowery, James 1837 rb-9-462

Lowry, Mary 1845 rb-13-222

Lucas, Oslin 1851 rb-16-33

Luckett, Davis sr. 1846 rb-13-633

Lyon, Wm. H. 1854 rb-17-329

Lyon, Elizabeth 1857 rb-18-438

Lyon, Elizabeth 1857 rb-18-607

Lyon, Nathan 1857 rb-18-390

Lytle, John 1841 rb-12-26

Lytle, Mary W. 1848 rb-14-217

Lytle, Sophia 1858 rb-19-489

Lytle, William sr. 1830 rb-8-110

Lytle, John 1841 rb-12-28

Lytle, Mary 1847 rb-14-204

Lytle, William 1829 rb-7-271

Mabry, John 1837 rb-10-19

Mabry, Peter A. B. 1848 rb-14-409

Mabry, Thomas J. 1826 rb-6-184

Mabry, Thomas J. 1855 rb-17-613

Macgowan, William B. 1848 rb-14-465

Macgowan, Ebenezer 1850 rb-15-346

Macklin, James 1820 rb-4-237

Maddox, Sarah 1851 rb-16-110

Maddox, Sarah H. 1851 rb-16-130

Madison, Ambrose 1842 rb-12-223

Mallard, John 1815 rb-3-51

Malloy, Gilliam 1814 rb-3-77

Malone, William N. 1847 rb-14-138

Malry, Thomas J. 1828 rb-7-45

Maney, Thomas H. 1847 rb-14-67

Mankin, Jeremiah 1858 rb-19-155

Mankin, William 1829 rb-7-172

Mankins, Hezekiah 1853 rb-16-625

Mankins, William 1850 rb-15-558

Manning, Edward 1815 rb-3-57

Manning, John 1823 rb-5-312

Manning, Mary A. P. 1858 rb-19-380

Manning, Parthena 1858 rb-19-292

Manning, William 1816 rb-3-142

Manor, Mills 1848 rb-14-487

Manor, Nancy 1847 rb-14-2

Marable, A. H. 1834 rb-9-119

Marable, Elizabeth 1841 rb-11-104

Marable, H. H. 1853 rb-16-399

Marable, Isaac 1831 rb-8-210

Marable, Isaac H. 1820 rb-4-245

Marable, Isaac M. 1829 rb-7-193

Marable, Elizabeth 1841 rb-11-110

Marable, Henry H. 1833 rb-9-72

Marable, Travis 1825 rb-6-168

Margowan, William B. 1848 rb-14-436

Marley, Robert 1806 rb-2-11

Marlin, William 1805 rb-2-5

Marshall, Daniel 1822 rb-5-177

Marshall, Alexander D. 1850 rb-15-345

Martin, James 1836 rb-9-350

Martin, John 1859 rb-20-47

Martin, Mary 1852 rb-16-319

Martin, Josias 1835 rb-9-263

Martin, Robert 1840 rb-11-52

Mason, Delita D. 1854 rb-17-274

Mason, Martha E. 1854 rb-17-274

Mason, P. M. 1858 rb-19-177

Mason, Pleasant 1857 rb-19-82

Mason, Coleman 1820 rb-5-13

Mason, Reynear H. 1852 rb-16-145

Mathews, William R. 1849 rb-15-117

Mathews, John 1843 rb-12-343

Mathis, James 1826 rb-7-326

Matthew, Dudly 1814 rb-2-283

Matthews, William 1823 rb-6-28

Maxwell, James J. 1829 rb-7-163

Maxwell, Jno. W. 1830 rb-8-411

Maxwell, James J. 1829 rb-7-278

May, John 1814 rb-2-303

May, Joseph 1849 rb-15-76

May, Robert 1857 rb-19-66

Mayfield, Thomas 1846 rb-13-710

Mayfield, Thomas F. 1848 rb-14-358

McAdoo, Erastus 1852 rb-16-223

McAdoo, Erastus Z. 1853 rb-16-573

McAdoo, Eratus B. 1852 rb-16-190

McAdoo, Joseph S. 1861 rb-21-142

McAdoo, Samuel 1847 rb-14-63

McAdoo, Mary 1860 rb-20-586

McAdoo, Samuel P. 1856 rb-18-88

McAlhatton?, Mary 1830 rb-8-97

McBride, Francis 1809 rb-2-83

McCaib, Andrew 1828 rb-7-93

McCartney, Margaret 1840 rb-10-508

McClanahan, Robert 1854 rb-16-716

McClanahan, Samuel 1847 rb-14-172

McClanahan, Sarah 1858 rb-19-383

McClane, Lewis 1856 rb-18-245

McClannahan, R. B. 1853 rb-16-709

McClaran, Jno. D. 1851 rb-16-109

McColloch, Sarah Ann 1854 rb-17-161

McCombs, Jane 1828 rb-7-157

McCombs, Robert 1825 rb-6-165

McConley, M. 1831 rb-8-174

McCorkle, William 1818 rb-4-118

McCoy, John 1815 rb-3-70

McCoy, Robert 1844 rb-12-430

McCoy, Sherod 1835 rb-9-197

McCoy, Beaty 1816 rb-3-118

McCoy, Sherard 1836 rb-9-162

McCracken, George 1826 rb-6-274

McCrae, William 1856 rb-17-638

McCrary, John 1856 rb-18-184

McCray, William 1857 rb-19-85

McCulloch, Robert 1844 rb-12-497

McCulloch, Samuel 1821 rb-5-84

McCulloch, Benjamin 1848 rb-14-242

McCulloch, Robert L. 1844 rb-12-498

McCullock, Samuel 1809 rb-2-72

McCullough, Alexander 1850 rb-15-479

McElhatten, Stewart 1855 rb-17-581

McElroy, James 1847 rb-14-170

McElroy, Jane 1848 rb-14-435

McElroy, John C. 1853 rb-16-650

McElroy, Samuel 1847 rb-14-221

McElroy, Adam C. 1846 rb-13-641

McEwen, Alexander 1827 rb-6-298

McEwen, Alexander 1853 rb-17-126

McEwen, Hannah 1852 rb-16-350

McEwen, Jas. A. 1854 rb-16-714

McEwen, John 1824 rb-6-67

McEwen, James 1815 rb-3-29

McFadden, Robt. W. 1840 rb-11-51

McFadden, Saml. 1848 rb-14-369

McFadden, Francis W. 1842 rb-12-258

McFarland, Sarah 1844 rb-12-489

McFarlin, Sarah 1854 rb-17-35

McFarlin, William 1837 rb-9-403

McFarlin, Benjamin 1829 rb-7-348

McFarlin, William 1824 rb-6-43

McFarling, Sarah M. 1856 rb-18-190

McFerren, John 1809 rb-2-68

McGill, Isaac 1848 rb-14-241

McGill, James 1834 rb-9-75

McGill, Nancy 1858 rb-19-285

McGill, Samuel 1833 rb-9-63

McGowan, Ebenezer 1852 rb-16-247

McGowan, Francis (Mrs.) 1853 rb-16-456

McGowan, Francis 1852 rb-16-336

McGowan, William B. 1854 rb-17-82

McGowen, Lucy 1861 rb-21-69

McGowen, Lucy A. 1859 rb-20-154

McGowen, T. H. 1859 rb-20-155

McGowen, Thomas H. 1861 rb-21-69

McGregor, John 1835 rb-9-270

McGregor, John 1847 rb-14-188

McGrigor, Milberry 1846 rb-13-465

McHenry, John 1823 rb-5-332

McIver, Evander 1828 rb-7-118

McIver, John 1830 rb-8-153

McIver, John 1840 rb-11-25

McIver, Evander 1828 rb-7-283

McKay, David 1837 rb-9-402

McKeen, J. H. 1831 rb-8-262

McKeen, John H. 1836 rb-9-114*

McKeen, Alexander 1825 rb-6-166

McKnight, Eliza Y. 1859 rb-20-152

McKnight, Ellenor 1848 rb-14-388

McKnight, John 1823 rb-5-327

McKnight, Samuel F. 1841 rb-12-52

McKnight, Samuel Folle 1841 rb-12-99

McKnight, Eleanor 1828 rb-7-337

McKnight, James 1822 rb-5-220

McKnight, William 1831 rb-8-328

McKnight, William 1840 rb-11-15

McLanahan, Sarah 1858 rb-19-524

McLaughlon, Joseph 1814 rb-2-300

McLean, Charles 1826 rb-6-260

McLean, Charles 1847 rb-14-203

McLean, Charles G. 1853 rb-16-672

McLean, Lewis 1854 rb-17-321

McLean, Sarah 1847 rb-14-202

McLean, William E. 1857 rb-18-626

McLin, James 1820 rb-4-259

McLin, John A. 1839 rb-10-360

McLin, Robert 1841 rb-11-205

McLin, Wm. E. 1852 rb-16-151

McMurry, Samuel 1827 rb-7-79

McMury, James 1829 rb-7-257

McPeak, Eliza A. 1857 rb-19-120

McPeak, James 1853 rb-16-651

McPeak, John 1853 rb-16-653

McRae, Wm. 1855 rb-17-529

McWhirton, S. C. (Dr.) 1856 rb-18-123

McWirter, S. C. 1856 rb-18-100

Mecklin, James 1820 rb-5-77

Medows, Ephraim 1852 rb-16-269

Michell, James 1854 rb-17-143

Miles, Hartwell 1840 rb-10-492

Miles, Thomas 1839 rb-10-311

Miles, Sarah A. 1862 rb-21-169

Miles, Thomas sr. 1838 rb-10-181

Miller, E. S. 1859 rb-19-569

Miller, Elizabeth 1854 rb-17-247

Miller, Hardy 1857 rb-19-42

Miller, Isaac J. 1841 rb-12-6

Miller, John 1805 rb-2-8

Miller, John 1847 rb-14-203

Miller, John A. 1847 rb-14-223

Miller, John R. 1859 rb-20-196

Miller, Lewis 1850 rb-15-414

Miller, Margaret 1833 rb-9-78

Miller, Mathew 1814 rb-1-167

Miller, Mathew 1837 rb-10-29

Miller, N. C. 1857 rb-19-18

Miller, Prudence 1806 rb-2-20

Miller, Robert 1857 rb-18-429

Miller, William N. 1857 rb-19-130

Miller, Isaac 1844 rb-13-7

Miller, Isaac 1851 rb-16-115

Miller, Isaac 1861 rb-21-141

Miller, James R. 1846 rb-13-606

Miller, John 1820 rb-4-227

Miller, Robert 1837 rb-10-43

Miller, William P. 1832 rb-8-501

Minter, Jeptha 1861 rb-21-93

Mitchel, Mary 1856 rb-18-92

Mitchell, Azariah 1855 rb-17-583

Mitchell, James 1856 rb-17-682

Mitchell, Robert 1853 rb-16-653

Mitchell, Wm. 1854 rb-16-712

Mitchell, James 1843 rb-12-344

Mize, Henry 1816 rb-3-141

Molloy, Fanny M. 1855 rb-17-529

Molloy, Gilliam 1830 rb-8-66

Molloy, Gwilliam 1817 rb-4-84

Molloy, William 1855 rb-17-360

Molloy, Fanny M. 1855 rb-17-533

Molloy, John 1857 rb-19-64

Montgomery, Joseph 1843 rb-12-289

Montgomery, Mary M. 1843 rb-12-385

Montgomery, Stepney 1858 rb-19-218

Montgomery, Hugh 1826 rb-6-251

Montgomery, Joseph A. 1840 rb-11-58

Montgumery, Stephen 1857 rb-19-126

Moody, Samuel 1816 rb-3-121

Moor, Samuel 1826 rb-6-216

Moore, Andrew K. 1858 rb-19-460

Moore, David 1846 rb-13-530

Moore, George T. 1837 rb-9-405

Moore, Isaac P. 1850 rb-15-418

Moore, James 1814 rb-2-252

Moore, John 1834 rb-9-86

Moore, John D. 1834 rb-9-186

Moore, John L. 1841 rb-11-310

Moore, Mary 1858 rb-19-512

Moore, Nancy 1842 rb-12-199

Moore, Robert 1838 rb-10-128

Moore, T. A. 1861 rb-21-158

Moore, Thomas 1847 rb-14-207

Moore, Walter O. 1837 rb-10-21

Moore, William 1844 rb-13-43

Moore, David 1822 rb-5-248

Moore, Isaac 1845 rb-13-227

Moore, James 1839 rb-10-411

Moore, Margaret 1825 rb-6-150

Moore, Martha R. 1858 rb-19-380

Moore, Noble 1857 rb-18-554

Moore, Noble 1860 rb-20-341

Morgan, Rolly 1861 rb-21-94

Morris, William 1846 rb-13-711

Morris, William 1820 rb-4-233

Morton, Catharine 1827 rb-7-119

Morton, Cicely 1842 rb-12-105

Morton, Francis M. 1839 rb-10-357

Morton, James 1847 rb-14-208

Morton, Joseph 1837 rb-9-410

Morton, Samuel 1842 rb-12-67

Morton, Samuel M. 1845 rb-13-387

Morton, Samuel sr. 1846 rb-13-580

Morton, Catharine 1827 rb-7-338

Morton, Cicely 1842 rb-12-116

Morton, James 1808 rb-2-64

Morton, James 1827 rb-8-1

Morton, Joseph 1823 rb-5-273

Morton, Nancy 1823 rb-5-336

Morton, Samuel 1846 rb-13-531

Morton, Solomon G. 1859 rb-20-75

Mosbey, John 1838 rb-10-84

Mosby, Jane 1833 rb-9-220

Moseby, David 1836 rb-9-286

Mosley, Samuel (Col.) 1805 rb-1-21

Muller, Lewis 1853 rb-16-665

Mullin, Joel 1836 rb-9-191

Mullins, Giles C. 1827 rb-7-109

Mullins, Jessee 1857 rb-18-316

Mullins, Jillis C. 1829 rb-7-180

Mullins, Joel 1835 rb-9-188

Mullins, John 1845 rb-13-223

Mullins, Oney 1842 rb-12-223

Mullins, Jesse 1842 rb-12-253

Murfree, Mary A. 1859 rb-20-145

Murfree, Mary Ann (Mrs.) 1857 rb-19-15

Murfree, Matthias B. 1854 rb-16-696

Murphey, Ezekiel 1843 rb-12-296

Murphey, John G. 1846 rb-13-465

Murphey, Wayne W. 1849 rb-15-2

Murphrey, Miles P. 1854 rb-17-137

Murphy, Wayne 1854 rb-17-36

Murphy, Wayne W. 1849 rb-15-38

Murray, Samuel 1847 rb-14-5

Murray, Thomas 1843 rb-12-418

Muse, Richard T. 1858 rb-19-379

Muse, Samuel 1847 rb-14-175

Muse, Samuel O. 1848 rb-14-485

Muse, Richard T. 1858 rb-19-317

Muse, William J. 1848 rb-14-433

Nance, A. W. 1855 rb-17-584

Nance, Allen 1848 rb-14-386

Nance, Isaac 1820 rb-4-247

Nance, Isham 1828 rb-7-23

Nance, Jane 1859 rb-19-571

Nance, Allen 1836 rb-9-327

Nance, Bird 1814 rb-3-110

Nash, John 1836 rb-9-313

Nash, Thomas 1828 rb-7-24

Naylor, W. H. 1857 rb-19-119

Naylor, Wade H. 1857 rb-19-234

Neal, Gracy 1857 rb-19-81

Neal, Gray 1858 rb-19-418

Neal, Thomas 1859 rb-20-204

Neal, John 1845 rb-13-146

Neal, William D. 1856 rb-18-231

Neblet, Elizabeth 1834 rb-9-117

Neel, Sarah E. 1857 rb-18-327

Neeley, John 1845 rb-13-418

Neeley, Nancy 1849 rb-15-36

Nelson, Benj. B. 1835 rb-9-247

Nelson, Benjamin A. 1834 rb-9-147

Nelson, Daniel 1845 rb-13-418

Nelson, Humphrey 1814 rb-2-248

Nelson, James C. 1860 rb-20-587

Nelson, Judieth 1851 rb-15-629

Nelson, Mary 1848 rb-14-389

Nelson, Mathew 1856 rb-18-211

Nelson, Pleasant H. 1831 rb-8-327

Nelson, Thomas 1851 rb-15-625

Nesbitt, Joseph 1857 rb-19-127

Nevel, John 1830 rb-8-226

Nevil, James 1831 rb-8-243

Newgent, William H. 1844 rb-12-488

Newgent, William H. jr. 1849 rb-14-509

Newgent, William jr. 1846 rb-13-714

Newman, Allen 1859 rb-20-82

Newman, James 1840 rb-11-50

Newman, John 1842 rb-12-106

Newman, John sr. 1844 rb-12-575

Newman, John 1842 rb-12-111

Newman, Joseph 1849 rb-15-204

Newsom, Thomas J. 1836 rb-9-306

Newsom, Sarah B. 1852 rb-16-334

Nichols, James 1852 rb-16-150

Nichols, Joseph 1826 rb-6-182

Nickson, William 1820 rb-4-232

Nisbett, Alexander sr. 1853 rb-16-356

Nisbett, Alexr. 1852 rb-16-323

Nivins, James 1852 rb-16-338

Nixon, John 1842 rb-12-238

Nixon, John B. 1842 rb-12-288

Noe, John 1859 rb-19-633

Nolen, Purce G. 1840 rb-11-55

Norfleet, Thomas N. 1835 rb-9-254

Norman, Carna S. 1853 rb-16-501

Norman, Isaac 1814 rb-2-292

Norman, James 1826 rb-6-212

Norman, John 1826 rb-6-194

Norman, Thomas 1828 rb-7-51

Norman, William 1814 rb-2-282

Norman, William 1828 rb-7-47

Norman, Carna H. 1850 rb-15-349

Norman, Elizabeth 1848 rb-14-244

Norman, Furney G. 1836 rb-9-99

Norman, John 1809 rb-2-66

Norman, Thomas 1828 rb-7-341

Norris, John 1815 rb-3-55

North, Theodrick 1860 rb-20-339

North, William 1845 rb-13-164

North, Theodrick 1860 rb-20-345

North, William 1833 rb-9-65

Northcott, Joel 1809 rb-2-76

Northcott, Martha S. 1851 rb-16-119

Northcutt, Martha 1854 rb-17-172

Northcutt, Hosea 1850 rb-15-486

Norvell, Nancy B. 1850 rb-15-321

Nowlen, P. G. 1857 rb-18-294

Oakley, William 1851 rb-15-619

Oden, Thomas A. 1827 rb-7-290

Ogilvie, Francis 1821 rb-5-81

Ogilvie, Smith 1812 rb-2-177

Oglevie, Smith 1822 rb-5-239

Oliphant, James 1849 rb-15-3

Oliver, Jane 1857 rb-19-27

Osborne, Elizabeth 1835 rb-9-268

Osborne, Phillips 1829 rb-7-182

Oslin, Lucus 1851 rb-15-568

Ott, John 1854 rb-17-1

Ott, R. B. 1857 rb-19-80

Overall, Andrew J. 1848 rb-14-380

Overall, Isaac 1857 rb-19-17

Overall, Isaac H. 1859 rb-19-537

Overall, Jackson 1846 rb-13-697

Overall, Jackson M. 1845 rb-13-388

Overall, James G. 1848 rb-14-325

Overall, Sarah E. 1854 rb-17-1

Overall, W. L. 1860 rb-20-704

Overall, Nathaniel 1835 rb-9-258

Overall, William S. 1858 rb-19-507

Overdeer, Jacob 1836 rb-9-383

Owen, Thomas 1844 rb-12-488

Owen, Thomas 1860 rb-20-341

Owen, Thomas 1860 rb-20-343

Pace, Briton 1825 rb-6-100

Pace, James 1815 rb-3-59

Pace, John 1815 rb-3-105

Page, William D. 1837 rb-10-8

Painter, John 1851 rb-15-569

Pallett, Abraham 1812 rb-2-172

Palmer, Ophelia M. 1856 rb-18-131

Palmer, William H. 1845 rb-13-180

Parker, Daniel 1815 rb-3-82

Parker, Daniel 1835 rb-9-241

Parker, Docton 1853 rb-16-643

Parker, Elizabeth 1858 rb-19-292

Parker, Isaac 1852 rb-16-341

Parker, John 1852 rb-16-241

Parker, Joseph 1850 rb-15-414

Parker, Joel 1836 rb-9-376

Parker, William 1842 rb-12-84

Parks, John 1830 rb-8-43

Parks, John 1845 rb-13-65

Parks, John 1830 rb-8-95

Parrish, George 1849 rb-15-17

Parrish, George W. 1833 rb-9-14

Patillo, H. H. 1834 rb-9-163

Patillo, Harrison 1833 rb-9-42

Patrick, James D. 1831 rb-8-326

Patrick, Jesse 1820 rb-5-50

Patterson, Alexander 1831 rb-8-214

Patterson, I. W. 1856 rb-18-32

Patterson, Isaac W. 1850 rb-15-440

Patterson, Jefferson W. 1854 rb-17-320

Patterson, Louvica 1853 rb-16-404

Patterson, Samuel 1848 rb-14-447

Patterson, Samuel 1860 rb-20-503

Patterson, James 1830 rb-8-164

Patterson, John 1856 rb-18-217

Pattillo, Littleton 1842 rb-12-106

Pattillo, Samuel 1841 rb-12-31

Pattillo, Littleton 1842 rb-12-115

Patton, Joseph C. 1856 rb-18-192

Patton, Samuel 1839 rb-10-269

Patton, Matthew 1808 rb-2-62

Paul, Asa 1818 rb-4-171

Payne, Andrew B. 1841 rb-12-36

Payne, Martha 1822 rb-5-223

Payne, Jacob 1847 rb-14-139

Peak, James M. 1857 rb-18-326

Peak, Simmons 1853 rb-16-438

Pearcy, Robt. W. 1853 rb-16-581

Pearcy, Thomas 1836 rb-9-360

Pearcy, Thomas T. 1836 rb-9-288

Pearson, David 1824 rb-6-52

Peck, James M. 1860 rb-20-646

Peck, Jeffery 1858 rb-19-489

Peck, Joseph 1847 rb-14-225

Peck, Simmons 1846 rb-13-585

Peek, Jeffery 1859 rb-19-571

Peek, Simmons 1845 rb-13-417

Peek, Jeffery 1850 rb-15-453

Peek, Joseph 1847 rb-14-166

Penn, George 1826 rb-6-227

Penn, Martha 1828 rb-7-151

Penn, Martha 1828 rb-7-324

Perkins, Joseph 1825 rb-6-157

Perkins, Mary 1823 rb-5-325

Petty, Charles 1860 rb-20-416

Peyton, John M. 1858 rb-19-319

Philips, Bennett 1853 rb-16-656

Philips, Joseph 1857 rb-19-78

Philips, James William 1854 rb-17-186

Phillips, Bennett 1842 rb-12-237

Pickins, Joseph 1820 rb-4-242

Pierce, Isaac 1847 rb-14-198

Pinckard, Bailey 1859 rb-20-112

Pinkard, William 1853 rb-16-464

Pitts, William 1852 rb-16-203

Pitts, William 1852 rb-16-213

Pivers, William 1825 rb-6-128

Poe, Jonathan 1818 rb-4-126

Pogue, Elizabeth 1841 rb-12-25

Pogue, James 1814 rb-1-164

Pogue, Martha 1814 rb-1-164

Poindexter, Joseph 1825 rb-6-139

Pointer, John 1851 rb-17-105

Pollard, Thomas P. 1816 rb-3-189

Pool, Alexander 1816 rb-4-3

Pope, C. 1860 rb-20-685

Pope, Charles 1860 rb-20-718

Posey, William S. 1854 rb-17-210

Posey, Zachariah 1844 rb-13-37

Potts, Henry 1838 rb-10-183

Potts, Henry 1852 rb-16-204

Powel, Rebecca 1827 rb-6-306

Powell, Charles 1857 rb-18-436

Powell, David 1817 rb-4-19

Powell, George W. 1816 rb-3-185

Powell, Rachel 1859 rb-20-83

Powell, Thomas 1859 rb-20-83

Powell, William 1826 rb-6-260

Prater, Elizabeth 1858 rb-19-384

Prater, Philip 1855 rb-17-582

Prewett, James M. 1837 rb-9-409

Prewett, John 1837 rb-10-25

Prewett, Smith 1837 rb-10-78

Price, John 1816 rb-3-218

Price, Francis Dennington 1830 rb-8-146

Price, John 1806 rb-2-16

Price, Robert C. 1852 rb-16-332

Prim, Abraham 1825 rb-6-105

Prim, Abram 1835 rb-9-208

Primm, James O. K. 1846 rb-13-464

Pritchett, Samuel 1853 rb-16-434

Puckett, Cas 1854 rb-17-264

Puckett, Elizabeth (Mrs.) 1860 rb-20-542

Puckett, Elizabeth 1859 rb-20-113

Puckett, Leonard 1842 rb-12-256

Puckett, Milly 1859 rb-20-235

Puckett, Arthur 1827 rb-6-308

Puckett, Charles 1854 rb-16-796

Puckett, Lodwick 1860 rb-20-414

Puckett, Nancy 1846 rb-13-687

Puckett, Nathaniel 1842 rb-12-177

Pullam, George W. 1840 rb-10-491

Pullen, Thomas 1821 rb-5-173

Pybas, Stephen 1839 rb-10-312

Qualls, George W. 1842 rb-12-83

Quarlles, John W. 1845 rb-13-159

Ragan, J. B. 1859 rb-20-205

Ragan, Jno. B. 1860 rb-20-412

Raines, Henry Y. 1838 rb-10-216

Rainey, John sr. 1856 rb-18-240

Rainey, William 1860 rb-20-591

Rainey, Allen 1831 rb-8-400

Rainey, John 1854 rb-17-224

Rainy, John 1854 rb-17-209

Ralph, Thomas 1837 rb-9-434

Ralston, Elizabeth 1854 rb-17-318

Ralston, George 1847 rb-14-160

Ralston, George 1858 rb-19-332

Ralston, George 1837 rb-10-31

Ramsey, David 1815 rb-3-54

Ramsey, William 1833 rb-9-84

Randolph, G. R. 1831 rb-8-278

Randolph, James A. 1859 rb-20-56

Randolph, Sarah 1858 rb-19-210

Randolph, Sarah J. 1852 rb-16-242

Randolph, Harrison 1835 rb-9-259

Randolph, Mary 1827 rb-7-329

Randolph, Peter 1856 rb-18-125

Rankin, Armina 1841 rb-11-109

Rankin, James P. 1832 rb-8-428

Rankin, Alexander 1835 rb-9-206

Rankin, David 1831 rb-8-190

Rankin, James 1844 rb-12-556

Ransom, Benjamin 1845 rb-13-186

Ransom, Elizabeth 1857 rb-19-42

Ransom, Gideon M. 1850 rb-15-487

Ransom, John 1849 rb-15-162

Ransom, Richard 1847 rb-14-56

Ransom, Benjamin C. 1844 rb-13-31

Ransom, William 1816 rb-3-146?

Rawlings, John 1840 rb-10-480

Rawlings, Sarah 1844 rb-13-30

Rawlings, Sarah R. 1848 rb-14-287

Rawlings, Thomas 1846 rb-13-715

Rawlings, William 1827 rb-7-2

Rawlings, William 1827 rb-7-347

Ray, Charles 1809 rb-2-77

Ray, Thomas 1849 rb-15-119

Read, Edmund R. 1856 rb-17-694

Read, Elijah 1845 rb-13-439

Read, Eliza 1845 rb-13-388

Read, John 1845 rb-13-214

Read, John N. 1836 rb-9-298

Read, John Nash 1853 rb-16-537

Read, Robert A. 1849 rb-15-32

Read, Robert H. 1848 rb-14-357

Read, William 1846 rb-13-523

Read, Edmund Randolph 1843 rb-12-413

Read, Edward Randolph 1856 rb-18-89

Read, James 1839 rb-10-464

Read, John Nash 1826 rb-6-179

Read, Mary 1856 rb-17-663

Read, Mary 1861 rb-20-743

Read, P. F. A. 1852 rb-16-290

Read, William B. 1843 rb-12-417

Ready, Charles sr. 1859 rb-20-148

Reed, John W. 1861 rb-21-49

Reed, R. A. 1848 rb-14-378

Reed, Thomas 1860 rb-20-642

Reeder, Mary D. 1859 rb-20-109

Reese, Mary 1849 rb-15-143

Reeves, John A. 1856 rb-18-234

Reeves, John C. 1856 rb-18-123

Reeves, Levi 1856 rb-18-215

Reeves, Moses G. 1861 rb-21-51

Reid, James 1820 rb-4-268

Renshaw, Isaah 1820 rb-4-269

Renshaw, Nathan 1849 rb-15-1

Renshaw, Nathan L. 1851 rb-15-614

Revel, Wilson 1850 rb-15-301

Revell, Isham 1836 rb-9-365

Rhodes, William 1815 rb-3-62

Richardson, David 1818 rb-4-109

Richardson, James 1826 rb-6-279

Richardson, James 1846 rb-13-694

Richardson, James F. 1842 rb-12-239

Richardson, James T. 1847 rb-14-29

Richardson, Mary 1840 rb-10-608

Richardson, William M. 1833 rb-9-47

Richmond, John 1810 rb-2-87

Ridley, George Granville 1860 rb-20-496

Ridley, Henry 1854 rb-17-320

Ridley, Henry jr. 1854 rb-17-169

Ridley, Moses 1854 rb-17-159

Ridley, Elizabeth 1858 rb-19-510

Ridley, Henry 1835 rb-9-233

Ridout, William 1833 rb-9-32

Robb, William 1859 rb-20-228

Robbins, Thomas 1832? rb-9-129

Roberson, William 1861 rb-21-9

Roberts, Cyrus 1844 rb-13-54
Roberts, Jesse 1838 rb-10-108
Roberts, Granville 1855 rb-17-535
Roberts, William 1812 rb-2-160
Robertson, Ezekiel 1844 rb-12-526
Robertson, H. 1860 rb-20-417
Robertson, James E. 1853 rb-16-465
Robertson, Thomas 1825 rb-6-136
Robertson, William 1858 rb-19-511
Robertson, Thomas 1831 rb-8-179
Robertson, William 1808 rb-2-36
Robertson, William B. 1839 rb-10-272
Robeson, Richard 1820 rb-4-239
Robinson, Frances 1837 rb-10-39
Robinson, Horace 1860 rb-20-467
Robinson, Isaiah 1859 rb-20-125
Robinson, Nancy L. 1844 rb-12-594
Robinson, Henry 1822 rb-5-209
Robinson, John H. 1841 rb-11-149
Robinson, Thomas 1830 rb-8-133
Rodgers, John 1839 rb-10-268
Rogers, Absalom 1839 rb-10-442
Rogers, David 1813 rb-2-239
Rogers, Joseph F. 1840 rb-11-64
Rollins, Thomas 1833 rb-9-39
Ross, Nancy 1854 rb-17-29
Ross, Wilson Y. 1850 rb-15-235
Ross, Robert 1845 rb-13-61
Roulhac, George 1840 rb-10-509
Roulhac, George G. 1839 rb-10-429
Roulhac, Francis 1852 rb-16-347
Rowlett, Rebecca 1858 rb-19-404
Rowlett, Rebecca J. 1858 rb-19-198
Rowlett, Thomas 1855 rb-17-516
Rowlett, Leonard S. 1851 rb-15-564
Rowlett, Thomas 1855 rb-17-536
Rowlon, Peyton 1859 rb-20-113
Rowlon, William 1859 rb-19-541
Rowten, William 1829 rb-7-317
Rowton, Molloy 1855 rb-17-532
Rowton, Peyton 1861 rb-21-3
Rowton, William 1856 rb-18-121
Rucker, Ann 1845 rb-13-416
Rucker, G. L. 1827 rb-6-337
Rucker, Gideon S. 1829 rb-7-178
Rucker, James 1830 rb-8-135

Rucker, Lavinia 1844 rb-12-584
Rucker, Mary Eliza 1856 rb-18-96
Rucker, Samuel C. 1823 rb-5-265
Rucker, Samuel C. jr. 1827 rb-6-289
Rucker, Thomas 1845 rb-13-222
Rucker, Williford 1845 rb-13-386
Rucker, Edmund M. 1859 rb-19-526
Rucker, James 1820 rb-4-199
Rucker, James 1850 rb-15-451
Rucker, Thomas sr. 1843 rb-12-309
Rushing, Joel A. 1844 rb-12-489
Russel, Melbry 1859 rb-20-155
Rutledge, John 1845 rb-13-416
Rutledge, Marcia H. 1854 rb-16-701
Sage, John 1827 rb-7-349
Sains, Noah 1854 rb-17-158
Sanders, Dollarson 1853 rb-16-672
Sanders, Donelson 1854 rb-16-719
Sanders, Edward F. 1847 rb-14-174
Sanders, J. J. 1845 rb-13-438
Sanders, John 1829 rb-8-42
Sanders, Levi L. 1855 rb-17-378
Sanders, Levi S. 1854 rb-17-191
Sanders, Philip 1840 rb-10-492
Sanders, R. D. 1858 rb-19-154
Sanders, Richard D. 1858 rb-19-269
Sanders, Robert 1855 rb-17-583
Sanders, Thomas 1807 rb-2-39
Sanders, Thomas 1845 rb-13-388
Sanders, Thomas W. 1860 rb-20-445
Sanders, Cornelious 1854 rb-16-799
Sanders, Isaac 1860 rb-20-436
Sanders, Philip 1823 rb-5-316
Saunders, Elihu 1844 rb-13-13
Saunders, J. James 1846 rb-13-640
Saunders, James 1844 rb-12-435
Saunders, T. W. 1859 rb-20-153
Saunders, Mary 1849 rb-15-37
Scarce, David 1854 rb-17-154
Scott, John T. 1849 rb-15-1
Searcy, Anderson 1845 rb-13-167
Searcy, Francis B. 1839 rb-10-312
Searcy, John W. 1844 rb-12-430
Searcy, Lafayette M. 1852 rb-16-279
Searcy, M. L. 1852 rb-16-240
Searcy, Richard 1804 rb-2-3

Searcy, Robert W. 1850 rb-15-558

Searcy, W. M. 1856 rb-18-23

Searcy, W. W. 1856 rb-19-224

Searcy, Anderson 1832 rb-8-419

Searcy, William W. 1846 rb-13-496

Sease, David 1852 rb-16-240

Seat, Margaret 1823 rb-5-337

Seats?, Peggy 1826 rb-6-215

Seward, John A. 1855 rb-17-551

Seward, Martha D. 1856 rb-18-189

Seward, Sarah P. 1849 rb-15-161

Seward, David 1848 rb-14-246

Seward, John 1854 rb-17-275

Sewell, Ezekiel 1853 rb-16-379

Sewell, Wm. 1851 rb-15-588

Shanklin, Robert D. 1846 rb-13-544

Sharber, Jehu 1845 rb-13-453

Sharber, John 1845 rb-13-225

Sharber, John E. 1860 rb-20-563

Sharp, Mary 1850 rb-15-480

Sharp, Rachel 1824 rb-6-60

Sharp, Robert 1849 rb-15-159

Sharpe, Cyrus 1826 rb-6-301

Sharpe, Theophilus A. 1831 rb-8-251

Sharpe, James 1811 rb-2-114

Sharpe, John 1825 rb-6-89

Shearwood, Hugh 1829 rb-7-306

Sheppard, Howarton 1820 rb-5-44

Sherwood, Benjamin 1826 rb-6-236

Ship, Joseph 1821 rb-5-133

Shipp, Benjamin 1850 rb-15-300

Shipp, Benjamin F. 1850 rb-15-362

Shipp, James sr. 1849 rb-15-51

Shute, Daniel 1849 rb-14-521

Simmons, Henry J. 1853 rb-16-649

Simpson, Hannah 1852 rb-16-192

Simpson, Robt. 1852 rb-16-192

Sims, George B. 1821 rb-5-138

Sims, Polly 1846 rb-13-530

Sims, Robert L. 1857 rb-18-439

Sims, Swepson 1850 rb-15-449

Singleton, Chappell 1848 rb-14-478

Singleton, Chapel H. 1848 rb-14-368

Slack, S. W. 1830 rb-8-103

Slandridge, Richard 1837 rb-9-440

Slate, Elizabeth 1839 rb-10-441

Sledd, John M. 1841 rb-12-44

Sledd, William 1827 rb-7-319

Smith, Cunningham 1840 rb-11-82

Smith, Edward W. 1815 rb-3-62

Smith, Elizabeth 1856 rb-17-611

Smith, Guy 1823 rb-5-288

Smith, Jackson 1861 rb-20-801

Smith, James 1828 rb-7-115*

Smith, James 1859 rb-20-46

Smith, James M. 1848 rb-14-338

Smith, James S. (B) 1858 rb-20-16

Smith, James S. 1841 rb-11-286

Smith, James S. 1858 rb-19-383

Smith, John B. 1850 rb-15-345

Smith, John E. 1850 rb-15-439

Smith, John T. 1855 rb-17-380

Smith, John W. 1837 rb-10-25

Smith, Joseph 1829 rb-7-173

Smith, Josiah 1816 rb-3-137

Smith, Martha A. 1854 rb-17-158

Smith, Mary 1839 rb-10-380

Smith, O. B. 1853 rb-16-467

Smith, Polemna 1835 rb-9-248

Smith, Robert 1806 rb-2-12

Smith, Robert 1849 rb-15-36

Smith, Robert sr. 1826 rb-6-259

Smith, Samuel 1809 rb-2-81

Smith, Samuel 1861 rb-21-84

Smith, Thomas 1835 rb-9-268

Smith, Thomas 1846 rb-13-694

Smith, William 1814 rb-2-273

Smith, William G. 1859 rb-20-196

Smith, William H. 1851 rb-15-565

Smith, Wm. A. 1853 rb-16-538

Smith, Ann 1821 rb-5-95

Smith, Bennett 1848 rb-14-372

Smith, Cecily M. 1862 rb-21-166

Smith, Ephraim F. 1856 rb-17-618

Smith, Isabella 1852 rb-16-339

Smith, James 1847 rb-14-206

Smith, John 1813 rb-2-214

Smith, John 1825 rb-6-116

Smith, John 1861 rb-21-103

Smith, John P. 1853 rb-17-271

Smith, Mary 1821 rb-5-93

Smith, Millington 1836 rb-9-380

Smith, Obadiah 1819 rb-5-10

Smith, Polly 1844 rb-12-588

Smith, Robert 1834 rb-9-170

Smith, Robert 1849 rb-15-52

Smith, Samuel 1851 rb-15-620

Smith, William 1833 rb-9-60

Smith, William G. 1859 rb-20-110

Smith, William M. 1850 rb-15-559

Smotherman, J. R. 1861 rb-20-744

Smotherman, John G. 1847 rb-14-171

Smotherman, Jonathan P. 1849 rb-15-51

Smotherman, John 1833 rb-9-48

Smotherman, Samuel 1842 rb-12-254

Snead, William 1835 rb-9-252

Sneed (Snell?), Charles E. 1853 rb-16-569

Sneed, John 1854 rb-17-323

Sneed, Lucy 1839 rb-10-356

Sneed, Charles E. 1838 rb-10-190

Snell, Hardy 1852 rb-16-229

Snell, Hardy T. 1850 rb-15-300

Snell, James 1838 rb-10-239

Snell, Sarah R. 1859 rb-20-304

Snell, Willis 1851 rb-15-587

Soape, William 1836 rb-9-354

Spain, Lucy 1861 rb-21-157

Spain, Stephen 1840 rb-10-519

Spain, Stephen 1840 rb-10-553

Span, William 1843 rb-12-385

Spence, Alanson 1860 rb-20-622

Spence, Alaxson 1860 rb-20-639

Spence, M. 1857 rb-19-74

Spence, Nancy 1860 rb-20-564

Spence, Marmon 1847 rb-14-62

Spence, Sarah 1857 rb-18-634

Spencer, Joseph 1818 rb-4-186

Spencer, Joseph 1833 rb-9-50

Spencer, Richard 1848 rb-14-218

Spencer, Britain 1830 rb-8-93

Sperry, Lewis 1838 rb-10-165

Squairs, Evington 1820 rb-5-15

St. Clair, Lavelle 1837 rb-10-6

St. Clair, Wm. 1855 rb-17-528

Stack, Simon W. 1826 rb-6-266

Standridge, Elizabeth 1841 rb-11-309

Statham, Charles 1826 rb-6-237

Statham, Robert 1856 rb-18-97

Statham, Charles 1826 rb-6-252

Statham, Jane 1850 rb-15-321

Staton, Elijah 1850 rb-15-323

Stegar, William 1842 rb-12-252

Stegar, Francis 1854 rb-16-700

Stephens, Mary 1813 rb-2-245

Stephens, Mary B. 1815 rb-3-38

Stephenson, John 1817 rb-4-57

Sterrett, William 1822 rb-5-211

Stewart, James 1826 rb-6-243

Still, William 1820 rb-4-213

Still, William 1820 rb-5-39

Stockard, John 1846 rb-13-510

Stockard, John 1830 rb-8-167

Stokes, Young 1845 rb-13-406

Stokes, Young 1857 rb-19-57

Stone, John 1844 rb-12-435

Stovall, John 1816 rb-3-131

Stovall, Leroy M. 1860 rb-20-642

Stroup, Jacob 1812 rb-2-205

Sublett, Volentine M. 1846 rb-13-529

Sublett, William A. 1839 rb-10-451

Sublett, George A. 1855 rb-17-497

Sugg, Elizabeth 1832 rb-8-502

Sugg, John H. 1833 rb-9-21

Sulivan, Patrick 1831 rb-8-245

Sullivan, James 1818 rb-4-144

Sullivan, James 1831 rb-8-230

Sullivan, Patrick 1817 rb-4-76

Summerhill, William 1857 rb-18-637

Summerhill, William L. 1858 rb-19-223

Summers, Geo. 1834 rb-9-149

Summers, George 1853 rb-16-398

Summers, Robert 1851 rb-15-567

Summers, Thomas 1852 rb-16-242

Summers, William 1844 rb-12-500

Sumner, Geo. D. 1852 rb-16-236

Sumner, John H. 1837 rb-10-23

Sutton, Edmund 1825 rb-6-120

Swan, Robert 1845 rb-13-116

Swan, Robert B. 1845 rb-13-205

Swinfield, Barton 1856 rb-17-633

Swink, Michael 1860 rb-20-589

Tarpley, James A. 1860 rb-20-387

Tarpley, Thomas 1861 rb-21-109

Tatum, Mark 1832 rb-9-12

Tatum, Jesse 1834 rb-9-79

Taylor, Goodwin 1841 rb-12-25

Taylor, Henry 1854 rb-17-126

Taylor, James 1851 rb-17-127

Taylor, James M. 1844 rb-13-11

Taylor, John 1839 rb-10-447

Taylor, John L. 1836 rb-9-347

Taylor, Jos. F. 1852 rb-16-295

Taylor, Joseph 1847 rb-14-65

Taylor, Martha E. 1857 rb-18-587

Taylor, Martha M. 1857 rb-18-639

Taylor, Matilda 1847 rb-14-38

Taylor, Robert 1846 rb-13-686

Taylor, Rolly M. 1856 rb-17-611

Taylor, George 1829 rb-7-312

Taylor, James 1820 rb-4-205

Taylor, James 1829 rb-7-278

Taylor, Vincent 1861 rb-21-16

Teer, Richard V. 1845 rb-13-413

Teeter, Stout B. 1837 rb-10-33

Tench, John R. 1835 rb-9-222

Tench, John R. 1853 rb-16-620

Tennison, Abraham 1825 rb-6-169

Thacker, Larkin 1855 rb-17-415

Thacker, Jeremiah 1803 rb-2-6

Thacker, Larken 1842 rb-12-107

Thining?, David 1815 rb-3-115

Thomas, Edward 1861 rb-20-802

Thomas, John 1825 rb-6-135

Thomas, Wilson 1856 rb-18-99

Thomas, Wm. 1832 rb-8-484

Thomas, John 1828 rb-7-322

Thompson, Abram 1821 rb-5-113

Thompson, David 1858 rb-19-291

Thompson, David S. 1850 rb-15-379

Thompson, Gideon 1824 rb-6-55

Thompson, Henry D. 1835 rb-9-266

Thompson, James 1845 rb-13-223

Thompson, John 1813 rb-2-230

Thompson, John 1854 rb-17-184

Thompson, Nancy 1854 rb-17-160

Thompson, Rebecca C. 1826 rb-6-239

Thompson, Sarah G. 1838 rb-10-134

Thompson, Virginia W. 1852 rb-16-236

Thompson, William L. 1836 rb-9-328

Thompson, Wm. 1836 rb-9-224

Thompson, Wm. M. 1855 rb-17-531

Thompson, James 1811 rb-2-150

Thompson, Jessee 1859 rb-19-563

Thompson, John 1827 rb-6-311

Thompson, John 1835 rb-9-183

Thompson, Joseph 1816 rb-3-103

Thompson, Joseph 1827 rb-6-310

Thompson, Mary 1858 rb-19-508

Thompson, Orvell 1830 rb-8-1

Thompson, Robert 1844 rb-12-544

Thompson, Susan C. 1856 rb-18-185

Thorn, Thomas 1847 rb-14-136

Thurman, Wiley 1860 rb-20-702

Thurman, Wiley 1847 rb-14-77

Tier, Nancy 1859 rb-20-130

Tier, Richard V. 1848 rb-14-318

Tilly, John 1807 rb-2-32

Tilman, Jacob 1821 rb-5-143

Tinch, Elizabeth 1853 rb-16-603

Tinch, E. P. 1853 rb-16-537

Tinch, John R. 1835 rb-9-173

Tinsley, Vernon 1854 rb-17-66

Todd, Benjamin 1854 rb-17-1

Todd, Fielding 1857 rb-18-326

Todd, Jeremiah 1848 rb-14-241

Todd, Robert 1860 rb-20-563

Todd, Robin 1861 rb-21-24

Todd, Aaron 1859 rb-20-118

Tombes, William 1829 rb-7-303

Travis, Amos 1839 rb-10-446

Travis, Amos F. 1832 rb-9-11

Travis, W. 1833 rb-9-92

Traylor, Joel 1859 rb-20-114

Traylor, Joel 1859 rb-20-149

Tribble, Eli 1842 rb-12-252

Trimble, Joseph 1858 rb-19-271

Truman, Miles 1815 rb-3-108

Tucker, Almira 1839 rb-10-463

Tucker, Claibourne L. 1849 rb-15-36

Tucker, Collins 1826 rb-6-262

Tucker, Daniel 1817 rb-4-94

Tucker, James 1815 rb-3-86

Tucker, James D. 1860 rb-20-621

Tucker, Joshua 1861 rb-21-148

Tucker, Kinchen 1861 rb-20-802

Tucker, Lavinia 1844 rb-12-489

Tucker, N. B. 1860 rb-20-340

Tucker, Saml. 1838 rb-10-118

Tucker, Samuel 1849 rb-15-60

Tucker, Sylvania 1842 rb-12-107

Tucker, William 1810 rb-2-100

Tucker, David 1836 rb-9-290

Tucker, James 1842 rb-12-256

Tucker, Jane K. 1844 rb-12-589

Tucker, Joshua C. 1861 rb-21-129

Turner, Joseph 1823 rb-5-327

Turner, E. B. 1856 rb-18-87

Tussell, John 1833 rb-9-78

Tweedy, Joseph 1813 rb-2-219

Twidy, Joseph 1823 rb-5-272

Twigg, Timothy 1845 rb-13-417

Underwood, Edmund 1836 rb-9-345

Underwood, Edwin 1836 rb-9-359

Underwood, John 1817 rb-4-79

Underwood, Levi S. 1833 rb-9-74

Underwood, William 1847 rb-14-52

Underwood, Levi S. 1836 rb-9-125

Vandike, William 1831 rb-8-401

Vardell, John 1815 rb-3-104

Vaughan, Drury 1827 rb-7-101

Vaughan, Elisha 1835 rb-9-225

Vaughan, Henry A. 1854 rb-16-714

Vaughan, John S. 1845 rb-13-386

Vaughan, Mildred L. 1844 rb-13-42

Vaughan, Peter R. 1841 rb-11-206

Vaughan, Peter R. 1854 rb-17-131

Vaughan, Richard 1850 rb-15-395

Vaughan, Richard B. 1855 rb-17-359

Vaughan, Sarah 1849 rb-15-281

Vaughan, William 1828 rb-7-35

Vaughan, William 1844 rb-12-589

Vaughan, William B. 1845 rb-13-224

Vaughan, A. W. 1860 rb-20-640

Vaughan, Drury 1827 rb-7-298

Vaughan, Henry A. 1854 rb-16-795

Vaughan, Sarah R. 1849 rb-15-78

Vaught, Simeon 1824 rb-6-56

Vawter, W. B. 1860 rb-20-737

Vernon, J. C. C. 1834 rb-9-118

Vernon, John C. C. 1834 rb-9-129

Vernon, Tinsley 1854 rb-16-713

Vinson, Rachell 1841 rb-12-44

Vinson, Henry 1841 rb-12-31

Wade, Ann 1845 rb-13-412

Wade, Ann 1858 rb-19-391

Wade, J. C. 1857 rb-18-612

Wade, James 1845 rb-13-224

Wade, John 1842 rb-12-233

Wade, Mary 1858 rb-19-384

Wade, Sarah 1856 rb-17-623

Wade, Thomas 1839 rb-10-430

Wade, Wilson L. 1857 rb-18-556

Wade, John C. 1856 rb-17-614

Wade, John sr. 1840 rb-10-488

Wade, Mary 1844 rb-12-487

Wade, Walter 1849 rb-15-140

Wade, William 1849 rb-15-134

Wadley, Samuel 1854 rb-17-30

Walden, John E. 1848 rb-14-389

Walker, Charles 1828 rb-7-28

Walker, James 1815 rb-3-56

Walker, John 1815 rb-3-73

Walker, William H. 1833 rb-9-75

Walker, Andrew J. 1850 rb-15-323

Walker, Martha 1841 rb-11-285

Walker, William 1835 rb-9-247

Walkup, Lewis M. 1857 rb-18-359

Wallace, John 1818 rb-4-125

Wallace, John 1834 rb-9-166

Wallace, John 1844 rb-12-576

Wallace, John sr. 1841 rb-11-212

Wallan, Joseph 1816 rb-4-2

Waller, Benjamin P. 1844 rb-12-499

Waller, Benjamin P. jr. 1846 rb-13-713

Waller, Benjamin 1818 rb-4-114

Waller, Benjamin P. 1844 rb-12-501

Wallis, John (Capt.) 1817 rb-4-5

Wallis, John 1824 rb-6-18

Walls, William 1823 rb-5-261

Walpole, John P. 1828 rb-7-10

Walpole, Charles 1851 rb-16-118

Ward, Benjamin 1860 rb-20-668

Ward, Best 1858 rb-19-460

Ward, Burrel 1856 rb-18-121

Ward, Ezekiel 1847 rb-14-134

Ward, Ezekiel jr. 1841 rb-11-284

Ward, Jesse 1853 rb-16-707

Ward, Mary 1852 rb-16-341

Ward, Robert 1847 rb-14-198

Ward, Thomas N. 1854 rb-17-210

Ward, Thomas S. 1852 rb-16-343

Ward, Thompson 1845 rb-13-65

Ward, William (Doctor) 1836 rb-9-304

Ward, William 1847 rb-14-166

Ward, Benjamin 1847 rb-14-176

Ward, Martha 1857 rb-18-633

Ward, Mary 1842 rb-12-178

Ward, William 1835 rb-9-215

Warren, Drury 1828 rb-7-30

Warren, John 1816 rb-3-218

Warren, John 1830 rb-8-78

Warren, John H. B. E. 1837 rb-9-404

Warren, John J. 1836 rb-9-361

Warren, Robert B. 1840 rb-10-490

Warren, William 1852 rb-16-311

Warren, John 1816 rb-3-226

Warren, Mary 1824 rb-6-1

Washington, Thomas 1833 rb-9-19

Washington, Thomas 1818 rb-4-167

Wasson, L. A. 1850 rb-15-363

Wasson, Logan 1856 rb-17-701

Wasson, Logan A. 1855 rb-17-459

Wasson, Logan H. 1850 rb-15-298

Wasson, Robert 1837 rb-9-435

Watkins, Fredrick 1830 rb-8-149

Watkins, Henry M. 1837 rb-9-426

Watkins, Roxana 1858 rb-19-401

Watkins, John M. 1859 rb-20-78

Watkins, Martha 1838 rb-10-229

Watkins, Richard 1836 rb-9-289

Watkins, Wilson L. 1861 rb-21-12

Weakly, Robert L. 1858 rb-19-236

Weatherly, Abner 1834 rb-9-211

Weatherly, Mary 1836 rb-9-203

Weatherspoon, Winfrey 1853 rb-16-402

Webb, Aaron 1855 rb-17-504

Webb, Hugh S. 1831 rb-8-301

Webb, Mahala 1857 rb-19-81

Webb, Mary 1852 rb-16-343

Webb, Elizabeth 1847 rb-14-80

Weger, Henry 1818 rb-4-138

Welch, Elizabeth 1846 rb-13-692

Welch, Thomas 1809 rb-2-82

Welch, Thomas 1843 rb-12-349

Wendel, David 1841 rb-11-293

Wendel, David 1844 rb-12-554

Wendel, David D. 1840 rb-11-57

West, Asa 1818 rb-4-175

West, George 1847 rb-14-107

West, Levi 1830 rb-8-220

West, George 1837 rb-10-1

Wheeler, Henry 1818 rb-4-159

White, Blumer 1821 rb-5-79

White, Henry 1856 rb-18-236

White, Levi sr. 1849 rb-14-522

White, Mary 1859 rb-20-241

White, Richard H. 1854 rb-17-322

White, Stokley N. 1848 rb-14-486`

White, Thomas 1811 rb-2-146

White, Wm. 1852 rb-16-322

White, Wm. W. 1852 rb-16-327

White, Levi 1848 rb-14-410

White, Stephen 1846 rb-13-532

Whitfield, Mathew 1827 rb-7-294

Whitly, Lewis 1816 rb-3-84

Whitmore, Gowen 1817 rb-4-61

Whitnel, Mary 1814 rb-2-288

Whitten, Stephen 1837 rb-9-441

Whoberry, Elizabeth 1821 rb-5-158

Wigger, Henry 1818 rb-4-151

Wilee, Thurman 1847 rb-14-181

Wilkinson, Hubbard S. 1845 rb-13-190

Wilks, William 1851 rb-15-600

Wilks, William H. 1849 rb-15-117

Willeford, Willis 1847 rb-14-83

Williams, Absolum 1812 rb-2-188

Williams, John 1815 rb-3-76

Williams, Wm. 1834 rb-9-165

Williams, David 1835 rb-9-178

Williams, Elisha jr. 1849 rb-14-500

Williams, Henry J. 1853 rb-16-564

Williams, John J. P. 1852 rb-16-291

Williams, Samuel 1806 rb-2-12

Williamson, Littleton 1835 rb-9-269

Williford, William 1816 rb-4-4

Williford, Willis 1846 rb-13-742

Wills, George 1851 rb-15-616

Wills, Macy 1860 rb-20-344

Willson, Nancy 1854 rb-17-272

Wilson, James H. 1847 rb-14-5

Wilson, John 1814 rb-2-272

Wilson, Saml. 1831 rb-8-192

Wilson, Saml. J. 1836 rb-9-281

Wilson, Saml. S. 1837 rb-10-42

Wilson, Thomas 1852 rb-16-341

Wilson, W. H. 1859 rb-19-567

Wilson, Wm. H. 1859 rb-20-38

Wilson, James 1817 rb-4-87

Windrow, Henry 1837 rb-9-424

Windrow, Henry 1826 rb-6-257

Wingo, Sarah (Miss) 1836 rb-9-313

Winn, John 1814 rb-2-298

Winston, Francis 1841 rb-11-205

Winston, Nathaniel 1856 rb-17-788

Witherspoon, Winfrey 1852 rb-16-191

Witherspoon, John 1841 rb-12-7

Wood, Ann 1853 rb-16-465

Wood, Elizabeth 1852 rb-16-237

Wood, George 1860 rb-20-407

Wood, John 1827 rb-8-53

Wood, John 1839 rb-10-301

Wood, Mary 1834 rb-9-145

Wood, Mitchel 1849 rb-14-521

Wood, Nancy 1844 rb-13-1

Wood, Orren L. 1835 rb-9-261

Wood, Owen L. 1836 rb-9-317

Wood, Susan 1851 rb-16-121

Wood, Thomas 1826 rb-6-300

Wood, William 1817 rb-4-60

Wood, William 1853 rb-16-673

Wood, George W. 1859 rb-20-239

Wood, Jesse 1835 rb-9-259

Wood, Nancy 1828 rb-7-336

Wood, W. W. 1853 rb-16-645

Woods, John 1815 rb-3-8

Woods, Lish 1859 rb-19-568

Woods, Syssily N. 1858 rb-19-427

Woods, Thomas C. 1846 rb-13-541

Woods, Nancy 1844 rb-13-38

Woolard, Thomas W. 1831 rb-8-221

Wooten, H. D. 1860 rb-20-642

Wooten, H. D. P. 1860 rb-20-678

Wooten, James W. 1854 rb-17-185

Word, Best 1859 rb-19-602

Word, Mary 1855 rb-17-494

Work, John 1835 rb-9-216

Work, John 1845 rb-13-147

Worke, Ann 1849 rb-15-107

Wrather, Asa 1843 rb-12-312

Wrather, Baker 1856 rb-18-118

Wray, Thomas 1840 rb-10-567

Wray, Thomas J. 1840 rb-10-490

Wright, Jacob 1861 rb-21-118

Wright, John 1857 rb-19-80

Wright, Thomas C. 1855 rb-17-414

Wright, Thompson 1834 rb-9-163

Wright, Francis 1808 rb-2-35

Wright, Isaac 1816 rb-3-228

Wright, Rebecca 1840 rb-10-579

Wright, William H. 1848 rb-14-393

Wynns, Bird 1848 rb-14-485

Yandell, Elizabeth 1840 rb-10-608

Yandell, William 1830 rb-8-46

Yandell, Wilson (Dr.) 1830 rb-8-11

Yandell, Elizabeth 1840 rb-10-625

Yandell, Willson 1828 rb-7-284

Yardley, Benjamin 1856 rb-18-237

Yardley, John W. 1855 rb-17-530

Yardley, Thomas 1849 rb-15-203

Yearby, William 1815 rb-3-54

Yearwood, Frederick 1821 rb-5-139

Yearwood, James 1853 rb-16-710

Yearwood, James P. 1854 rb-16-726

Yearwood, John 1822 rb-5-204

Yearwood, John 1847 rb-14-6

Yearwood, William 1823 rb-6-27

Yearwood, John 1847 rb-14-66

Yoes, John 1823 rb-5-328

Youree, Francis 1853 rb-16-617

Youree, Francis A. 1853 rb-16-403

Youree, James sr. 1835 rb-9-208

Youree, Joseph 1840 rb-10-478

Youree, Susan 1858 rb-19-209

Youree, Susannah 1857 rb-19-125

Youree, David 1834 rb-9-146

Youree, James 1845 rb-13-389

Yous, John 1821 rb-5-161

Zachary, Allen 1858 rb-19-355

Zachary, Josiah 1858 rb-19-354

Zachary, Malkigah 1858 rb-19-354

Zachery, Joshua 1830 rb-8-413

Zachry, Elizabeth 1840 rb-10-581

Zachry, Sarah B. 1840 rb-10-477

www.ingramcontent.com/pod-product-compliance
Lightning Source LLC
Chambersburg PA
CBHW050357100426
42739CB00015BB/3433